REFLECTIONS ON REGIONALISM
REPORT OF THE STUDY GROUP ON INTERNATIONAL TRADE

JAIME SERRA, CHAIRMAN

GUILLERMO AGUILAR

JOSÉ CÓRDOBA

GENE GROSSMAN

CARLA HILLS

JOHN JACKSON

JULIUS KATZ

PEDRO NOYOLA

MICHAEL WILSON

CARNEGIE ENDOWMENT FOR INTERNATIONAL PEACE

382
R332

Reflections on Regionalism:
Report of the Study Group on International Trade
may be ordered ($7.95) from Carnegie's distributor,
The Brookings Institution Press,
Department 029, Washington, D.C. 20042-0029, USA.
Tel. 1-800-275-1447 or 202-797-6258.
Fax 202 797-6004.

Edited by Valeriana Kallab.
Design by Paddy McLaughlin Concepts & Design.
Printed by Automated Graphic Systems.

Library of Congress Cataloging-in-Publication Data
Carnegie Endowment Study Group on International Trade
REFLECTIONS ON REGIONALISM:
Report of the Study Group on International Trade
Serra, Jaime (1951-   ), et al.
p. 84
ISBN: 0-87003-076-0

CONTENTS

PREFACE

In the fall of 1995, Morton Abramowitz and Moisés Naím invited me to chair a Study Group on International Trade, under the auspices of the Carnegie Endowment for International Peace—whose many past valuable contributions to the study of international affairs include sponsorship of Jacob Viner's seminal work (1950) on customs unions, a study of particular relevance to the theme of this report. After eight years in government, I was just returning to academia, as The Weinberg Visiting Professor at Princeton University's Woodrow Wilson School, and I was attracted by the opportunity that such a Study Group could provide to bring together policy-makers and academics to analyze some of the most important trade issues of our time. Moreover, my experience in the negotiation of various regional trade agreements and their world-wide proliferation had convinced me of the urgent need for further study of the issue of regionalism and its impact on the World Trade Organization.

Two natural candidates for the Study Group were my former counterparts in the negotiation of the North American Free Trade Agreement (NAFTA)—Carla Hills, former U.S. Trade Representative, and Michael Wilson, former Minister of Trade of Canada—with whom I had spent many hours discussing the impact of such agreements. Throughout the NAFTA negotiations, we had repeatedly shared our conviction that regional trade agreements must be fully compatible with multilateral rules; this was the fundamental premise on which we subsequently chose to base the work of the Carnegie Endowment Study Group. The Study Group offered us the rewarding experience of meeting again and analyzing these issues from a new standpoint—with each of us now working as a private consultant and thus able to pool thoughts from the same side of the table.

We decided to begin with a study of the theoretical implications of preferential agreements and their potential implications for trade and investment diversion. We would then review existing empirical analysis of different agreements to give our assessment of whether these agreements have had any negative effects on multilateral trade. Finally, after finding that neither theory nor empirical work yields an unambigious result as to whether these types of trade arrangements harm or help multilateral trade—we decided to identify the multilateral rules for regional agreements that could minimize their harmful and maximize their beneficial effects.

We were fortunate to be joined in the group effort by six outstanding individuals—lawyers and economists, each an expert on trade issues and on regional trade agreements in particular.

Guillermo Aguilar, now a senior partner at SAI (Law & Economics Consulting) in Mexico City, had been Mexico's Chief Counsel in the NAFTA negotiations and had co-drafted the text of that treaty. His participation in the Study Group was particularly helpful in the analysis of GATT's Article XXIV and the institutional issues involved in the relationship between the WTO and regional agreements. He also made an invaluable contribution to drafting the Study Group's policy recommendations and the Report itself.

José Córdoba, now a private consultant in Mexico, was a key figure in the Mexican government during the NAFTA negotiations and subsequently worked as a consultant to the World Bank, where he conducted comprehensive research on NAFTA's rules of origin. The Study Group was able to incorporate the main results of his research in suggesting the application of conditionality to the rules of origin in free trade agreements.

Gene Grossman, Jacob Viner Professor of Economics at Princeton University, is a leading authority on trade theory. His knowledge and deep understanding of preferential agreements is reflected in the theoretical and empirical reviews set out in this Report, as well as in the policy recommendations to avoid trade and investment diversion.

John Jackson, H. E. Yntema Professor of Law at the University of Michigan, is a distinguished trade law expert. His knowledge of the historical and legal aspects of multilateral and regional agreements provided useful background for the Study Group's discussions and the drafting of the Report, particularly on the legal implications of the policy recommendations.

Julius Katz, a distinguished U.S. trade negotiator and key player in the NAFTA negotiations, is now President of Hills & Company. His knowledge and experience on trade issues—in particular his wise analysis of the long-term nature of our policy recommendations—was invaluable.

Pedro Noyola, a former Mexican Under-Secretary of Trade and Finance, was instrumental in the negotiation of several free trade agreements and is now a senior partner at SAI (Law & Economics Consulting) in Mexico City. His deep knowledge of trade and investment policy issues contributed greatly to the dynamics of the group, the design of the policy recommendations, and the drafting of the Report.

The role that the World Trade Organization (WTO) will play on the international stage is in the process of being defined. As the world moves toward an increasingly global economy, new tensions are emerging that should be contained within clear and comprehensive institutional arrangements and rules designed to minimize trade and investment diversion. Our Report is a collective effort by a group keenly aware of the importance of mapping the right course at this crucial time. The five main recommendations that we make do not necessarily require immediate implementation; in our view, however, they represent an agenda that needs debate and analysis now, with a view to driving forward-looking decisions to ensure compatibility between regional trade agreements and the WTO.

We are particularly grateful to Peter Rodriguez for his very able research assistance, to Kristin McCarthy for her efficient handling of the logistics of the Study Group, and to all members of the Princeton University Workshop on Current Trade Issues for their research on the topic. We are much indebted to Anders Åslund, Jagdish Bhagwati, Avinash Dixit, Robert Fisher, Isaiah Frank, Peter Kenen, Denyse MacKenzie, Gary Sampson, and Joanna Wright for their comments and suggestions. We also wish to thank Valeriana Kallab for her editorial advice and for guiding the Report through to publication. Final responsibility for the views expressed of course rests with the authors.

Jaime Serra
Chairman
Study Group on International Trade

December 1996

SUMMARY OVERVIEW

Over the last three decades, regional trade agreements (Rtas) have proliferated to the point that, by 1995, virtually all members of the newly formed World Trade Organization (WTO) belonged to an RTA of some kind—mostly a customs union, a free trade agreement, or an interim agreement leading to one or the other. This development has greatly changed the world trade scene and represents both an important challenge and a unique opportunity for the new WTO: a challenge because RTAs can result in trade and investment diversion leading to high welfare *costs* for non-participants; an opportunity because they may create regional dynamic forces in favor of freer trade which, in turn, can generate important welfare *benefits* for the rest of the world.

The phenomenon of "regionalism" has emerged in the context of very rapid growth in world trade. Over the past 50 years, while world income has risen sixfold, real world trade has increased twelvefold. Over the last 20 years, foreign direct investment has multiplied twelvefold. Among the causes of these developments, trade and investment liberalization *policies* have played a very significant role. Trade liberalization has taken place at both the unilateral and multilateral levels. Market-oriented economic national reforms have consistently encompassed ambitious unilateral programs to eliminate trade and investment barriers; these have facilitated the access of goods, services, and new foreign investment, leading in turn to new trade and investment flows. At the multilateral level, moreover, further trade liberalization measures have been introduced after the conclusion of each of four rounds of trade negotiations under the General Agreement on Tariffs and Trade (GATT), which have also generated additional trade flows.

While the recent creation of many RTAs marks progress on liberalization policies within particular regions, it can constrain potentially broader benefits from liberalization under multilateral arrangements. In the early 1990s, RTA formation gained momentum for a variety of economic and institutional reasons. On the economic front, many of the smaller, more protectionist countries took it upon themselves to implement comprehensive trade liberalization reform programs. Unilateral liberalization became relevant in RTA creation to the extent that the smaller countries needed to complement internal efficiency gains from trade with external market access. Trade among "natural," already firmly established, trading partners intensified dramatically. On the institutional front, unilateral liberalization was taking place concurrently with the launching of the Uruguay Round of GATT negotiations (1986-94). Early on, that round was held up in extremely complicated negotiations, in part because of the ambitious agenda defined from the outset; reaching consensus on many of the issues became a cumbersome exercise with numerous political obstacles. Regional initiatives emerged from the midst of this political quagmire—as "safe havens" for many smaller countries that could not afford a "wait and see" strategy in the multilateral arena. By 1995, more than 50 percent of world trade was estimated to take place within RTAs.

Analysts are divided about the effects of these regional trade agreements. Some believe that taking further steps in the direction of trade and investment liberalization—even when restricted to a particular region—contributes to the creation of world trade and investment. Others believe that the implicit discrimination that these agreements embody diverts rather than creates worldwide trade and investment. Both sides of the debate have legitimate arguments.

Existing *theoretical* analysis—examined in this Report—leads to ambiguous conclusions. Economic theory alone cannot tell us whether RTAs are likely to increase or reduce distortions in the world trading system. From a static perspective, RTAs are more likely to enhance than to reduce world efficiency if their primary effect is to create new investment and trade rather than to divert existing investment and trade. The prospects for this depend upon existing trading patterns among would-be RTA members and the way in which the agreement is structured.

RTAs must be structured so as to *minimize* their potential for trade and investment diversion. In practice, this means ensuring that the common external tariffs of a customs union or the rules of origin of a free-trade agreement do not increase distortions in trade with the rest of the world. From a dynamic perspective, the key question is whether RTAs promote or retard further liberalization at the multilateral level, where it generates efficiency and other benefits for many more countries. Not much is yet known about which outcome is more likely, but the WTO must be ever-vigilant that RTAs not be used in a discriminatory way, as substitutes for global agreements.

The *empirical* analysis available—reviewed in detail in this Report—also leads to ambiguous results. Most studies suggest the same conclusions as the theory: RTAs do not necessarily bring harm to non-member countries, but they are not necessarily benign.

Since neither trade theory nor empirical analysis demonstrates conclusively what the trade- and investment-diverting effects of RTAs will be, the possibility remains that RTA proliferation may generate trade and investment diversion. This is why—50 years after the creation of the GATT—it is important that the WTO oversee the formation of these alliances to ensure that the agreements are structured in ways consistent with the broader goals of the world trading community. The trends toward regional integration need to be harnessed as a force for global liberalization.

The WTO should be better equipped to prevent trade and investment distortions that might constrain the emergence of a more efficient liberal multilateral trading system. Existing multilateral trade rules under the WTO umbrella and rules on investment under various agreements and WTO codes are either incomplete or dispersed and overlapping.

This Report makes several policy recommendations to improve the existing rules for regional agreements and thus to promote trade- and investment-creation.

Recommendation 1: Article XXIV of the GATT establishes the conditions on the basis of which member countries may form either a customs union (CU) or a free-trade agreement (FTA); these conditions, written in 1947 and subject to subsequent formal Understandings, still remain unsuitable for the current nature of regional trade agreements. *We recommend that the WTO adopt a new Understanding on Article XXIV that more precisely formulates the conditions on which countries may form an RTA—in particular with regard to tariffs and rules of origin. We believe that RTAs should move in the direction of a minimum external tariff. We also recommend that the transparency and enforcement of these new conditions be improved.*

Recommendation 2: Members in an RTA should harmonize their trade rules (e.g., antidumping regulations). We recognize that such harmonization may require a long transition period, during which time the use of rules to identify the origin of a product (national non-preferential rules of origin) will be required. However, such rules of origin should be implemented with care that they not create unnecessary obstacles to trade.

Recommendation 3: The WTO should develop a model accession clause to be included in all RTAs. Such a clause should list the set of disciplines that a new member must meet prior to entering into accession negotiations (e.g., the binding of its actual tariff schedule, compliance with any outstanding WTO final panel reports). Meeting these conditions should entitle the aspiring member to initiate negotiations.

Recommendation 4: Recognizing the linkages between trade and investment, we recommend that the WTO establish comprehensive multilateral investment rules for WTO members to adhere to on a voluntary basis.

Recommendation 5: The WTO should use its institutional structure and procedures to actively promote compatibility between regional trade agreements and the WTO itself. We make recommendations regarding the monitoring of compliance with our proposed new Understanding of Article XXIV (Recommendation 1), forum selection for dispute settlement, the establishment of rosters of panelists for dispute settlement, and the issuance of WTO rulings.

These recommendations provide an ambitious agenda. They are offered as guidelines for future WTO decisions and actions. Clearly not all of them can be implemented immediately. But unless changes of this nature are initiated very soon, preferential regional trade and investment liberalization and the establishment of regional monitoring institutions will continue to pose a serious challenge to the WTO's ability to protect and advance the interests of all participants in world trade.

The WTO should adjust its rules for the formation of RTAs, establish comprehensive multilateral investment rules, and address the relationship between regional and multilateral institutions. This Report also elaborates on the role that the WTO Committee on Regionalism should have on this agenda.

I. INTRODUCTION

Over the past three decades, regional trade agreements (RTAs) have proliferated to the point where virtually all members of the World Trade Organization (WTO) belong to some form of RTA notified to the GATT—whether a customs union, a free trade agreement, or an interim agreement leading to one or the other.[1] This development has redefined the world trade scene and represents both an important challenge and a unique opportunity for the WTO: a challenge because RTAs can result in trade and investment diversion, leading to high welfare *costs* for non-participants as well as for participants; an opportunity because they may create or strengthen regional dynamic forces in favor of freer trade, which can generate important welfare *benefits* for participants and for the rest of the world.

2. The WTO cannot rely solely on independent initiatives on the part of RTA members to build into their agreements the necessary conditions to avoid trade and investment diversion. It should exercise leadership to minimize such potential negative effects and to ensure that RTAs are effective building blocks of a more open multilateral system. Unfortunately, the WTO lacks adequate instruments with which to do so. Although Article XXIV of the General Agreement on Tariffs and Trade (GATT) has been somewhat strengthened through the Understanding that resulted from the Uruguay Round, it still remains insufficient to guarantee the consistency of RTAs with the liberalization of multilateral trade.

3. The purpose of this Report is to present some policy recommendations to the WTO aimed at strengthening its leadership role in dealing with RTAs. Vigorous leadership by the WTO is nec-

---

[1] In this Report, we use "regional" to refer to all preferential trade agreements—whether or not their member countries are geographically proximate. We also refer only to RTAs that have been notified to the GATT.

1

essary to minimize the risk of trade and investment diversion resulting from RTAs and to induce trade- and investment-creating behavioral patterns for existing and future RTAs.

4. Section II of this Report identifies the causes of the proliferation of RTAs, explains their nature and main characteristics (contrasting customs unions and free-trade areas), and identifies the risks and opportunities that such preferential arrangements present to the world trading system.

5. Section III presents the theoretical issues raised by preferential agreements, reviewing both the comparative static effects and the internal dynamics of RTAs and their consequences for trade and investment flows with the rest of the world. A distinction is made between the role played by the common external tariffs established by customs unions (CUs) and the rules of origin established by free-trade agreements (FTAs). These variables are crucial to understanding trade and investment diversion.

6. Section IV presents a brief review of empirical evidence of the effects of RTAs on trade flows within different RTAs and between RTAs and the rest of the world. Although it is difficult to distinguish between global and regional trade growth, different exercises are performed to isolate evidence of trade diversion.

7. Section V proceeds on the assumption that negative effects *could* occur and analyzes the existing multilateral rules for dealing with the risk of diversion. A detailed analysis of GATT Article XXIV and other enabling mechanisms for preferential treatment is presented. The Report highlights the inadequacy of existing provisions for managing RTAs in the world trading system—a system that bears little resemblance to the one that existed when Article XXIV was conceived.

8. Section VI sets out three different types of policy recommendations:

(a) Changes to Article XXIV and proposals for accession provisions and trade rules intended to minimize the risk of trade diversion;

(b) A policy roadmap for the WTO outlining multilateral investment rules to: (i) avoid investment diversion effects from both RTAs and other investment treaties, and (ii) create the necessary conditions for growing flows of foreign direct investment; and

(c) Institutional changes intended to ensure adequate monitoring and enforcement of the new WTO rules regarding RTAs.

9. An extensive selected bibliography on the subject of regionalism and its implications for the WTO is also provided for interested readers.

II. THE GROWING IMPORTANCE OF RTAS

RTAs have been an integral part of the world trading system throughout the GATT's history. It was clear to the original signatories of the GATT that British support for the Agreement was essential but also impossible without some flexibility regarding the terms of the 1932 Commonwealth of Nations Agreement. Similarly, over time, the formation of the Benelux Customs Union, of the European Coal and Steel Community, and of its successor, the European Economic Community (EEC), compelled the GATT to recognize special economic and political relationships in order to preserve its efficacy as a multilateral agreement. These exceptions to basic GATT methodology were contentious issues that presented challenges and prompted systemic adjustments. Concern about the EEC's external tariff and the Common Agriculture Policy of production subsidies was among the catalysts of the Dillon and Kennedy Rounds of GATT negotiations (1960-61 and 1964-67, respectively).

11. RTAs were originally accepted as exceptional derogations from the GATT's most-favored-nation (MFN) principle (Article I, see box). Today, they are customary arrangements that have grown in significance. Every major trading partner of the newly formed WTO but Hong Kong, Japan, and Korea is now a party to at least one regional economic agreement notified to the GATT. (Even these three countries are parties to a regional trade arrangement, the Asian and Pacific Economic Community (APEC), which, however, has not been notified to the GATT). RTAs are as diverse as they are numerous. While they generally fall into the categories of customs unions (CUs) or free-trade areas (FTAs), such agreements can look very distinct in the context of different sets of countries, different stages of development, different trading patterns, and different levels of commitment to trade liberalization.

> ## Article I. General Most-Favored-Nation Treatment
>
> 1. With respect to customs duties and charges of any kind imposed on or in connection with importation or exportation or imposed on the international transfer of payments for imports or exports, and with respect to the method of levying such duties and charges, and with respect to all rules and formalities in connection with importation and exportation, and with respect to the application of internal taxes to exported goods, and with respect to all matters referred to in paragraphs 2 and 4 of Article III, *any advantage, favor, privilege or immunity granted by any contracting party to any product originating in or destined for any other country shall be accorded immediately and unconditionally to the like product originating in or destined for the territories of all other contracting parties. . . .*

Note: Excerpt only; italics added. The text of this Article and all others cited in this Report is taken from GATT Secretariat, *The Results of the Uruguay Round of Multilateral Trade Negotiations*, June 1994.

12. Most RTA formation has occurred in two bursts of activity: first, during the 1960s and 1970s, and then again since 1990 (see Figure 1). The earlier growth was concentrated almost exclusively in Europe. Some 58 RTAs were signed and notified to the GATT between 1960 and 1979; and of those, at least 48 involved European signatories. The second era began at the end of the 1980s. Between 1990 and 1994 alone, over 30 agreements were notified to the GATT. Western Europe continues to be important in the formation of regional agreements. The primary impulse behind the recent European activity has been the breakup of the Soviet bloc; Central and Eastern European countries seek to form RTAs with the Euro-

Figure 1. Number of Regional Agreements Notified to the GATT

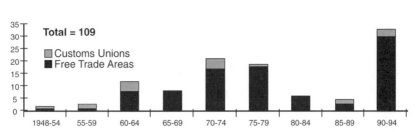

Source: WTO (1995).

pean Union (EU) and the European Free Trade Agreement (EFTA) countries as a way of securing markets and structuring their economic relations with one another. Less numerous but significant new regional agreements have also come about in the Americas, with the establishment of NAFTA and the Mercosur customs union between Argentina, Brazil, Paraguay, and Uruguay, and they are emerging more tentatively in Asia. The 51 reciprocal, GATT-notified RTAs in force in 1995 include dynamic and potentially expanding agreements such as the EU and NAFTA.

13. Regionalism began to gain momentum in the late 1980s for a variety of economic and institutional reasons. On the economic front, many smaller, more protectionist countries took it upon themselves to implement comprehensive trade-liberalizing reform programs. Unilateral liberalization became relevant for the formation of regional trading arrangements to the extent that these smaller countries needed to complement internal efficiency gains from trade with external market access. Trade among "natural" partners (i.e., countries already conducting a considerable amount of trade with one another) intensified dramatically. On the institutional front, unilateral liberalization was concurrent with the launching of the Uruguay Round of GATT negotiations (1986-94). Early on, the Round was held up in extremely complicated negotiations, in part due to the ambitious agenda defined at the outset. Reaching consensus on many of the issues became a cumbersome exercise that faced numerous political obstacles. Indeed, the Round faced near-collapse on many occasions. Regional initiatives emerged from the midst of this political quagmire—as safe havens for many smaller countries that could not afford a "wait and see" strategy in the multilateral arena.[2] But regional initiatives were not merely substitutes for multilateral negotiations; they also served an important role as complementary policy instruments of the larger players in the Uruguay Round, who sometimes used these initiatives to influence the multilateral negotiations.

14. The RTAs that grew out of the Uruguay Round significantly reduced trade barriers among many countries. Their influence on the course of global trade policies was equally important. To the extent that an RTA liberalizes markets or introduces trade "disciplines" beyond those embodied in other regional or multilateral agreements, it serves

---

[2] See Ethier (1996) for the opposite argument.

Figure 2. A Rough Estimate of World Trade within RTAs, 1995[3]

Trade within RTAs 53% $5,433 bil.

Other World Trade 47% $4,805 bil.

Source: IMF (1995) and WTO (1995).

as a model and testing ground for future agreements. In addition, it may generate support for deeper "plurilateral" and multilateral trade liberalization. The North American Free Trade Agreement (NAFTA) is a case in point. Despite concerns expressed at the time that NAFTA would divert attention away from MFN liberalization, it can be argued that NAFTA's successful negotiation in 1992 had a significant impact on stimulating trade liberalization efforts elsewhere. NAFTA helped rejuvenate the then-stalled Uruguay Round, and it encouraged nations in the Asia-Pacific region to adopt a set of principles to liberalize trade and investment between the years 2010 and 2020. Finally, NAFTA impelled the nations of the Western Hemisphere to agree to establish a hemispheric FTA by the year 2005.

15. At the same time it must be noted that NAFTA has stimulated a series of overlapping bilateral and plurilateral agreements within the Hemisphere. These agreements are classified as RTAs, but they are diverse in their terms and in the numbers of exceptions they contain. Their sometimes incomplete coverage raises the question of whether they should more properly be regarded as preferential agreements rather than true free-trade agreements. Whether these agreements will on balance create trade rather than divert it remains to be seen. More important, it is too soon to assess

---

[3] In the absence of detailed information, these figures were estimated by subtracting from total world trade the trade of all countries that do not belong to RTAs or the WTO. Total trade within RTAs was then calculated as the product of intra-regional trade shares (WTO, 1995) and total RTAs trade. It is assumed here that all intra-RTA trade is conducted on preferential terms.

their impact on broader trade liberalization, both multilateral and regional, through agreements such as the proposed Free Trade Area of the Americas.

16. Dedicated defenders of free trade are divided in their views on RTAs' effects on global welfare. Some argue that RTAs are beneficial institutions that complement WTO objectives. Others see them as serious impediments to globalism. Perhaps the basis of this division among professionals lies in the unresolved debate surrounding the legitimacy of RTAs as welfare-enhancing institutions. This lack of a consensus persists despite many theoretical and empirical contributions to the study of RTAs. The following sections of this Report provide an assessment of the theoretical as well as the empirical analysis of the effects of RTAs on trade and investment, and then conclude with an evaluation of WTO rules governing the establishment of RTAs. Suggestions to enhance and add to WTO policies are made throughout these sections.

III. THEORETICAL ISSUES

TRADE AND INVESTMENT

RTAs reduce or eliminate trade barriers among participating countries. It would appear, therefore, that such agreements represent a movement in the direction of freer world trade. However, it has been recognized—at least since the seminal writings of Jacob Viner (1950)—that the reality is more complex. While RTAs remove distortions in trade among member countries, they may introduce new distortions in trade between members and the outside world. These distortions arise from the *preferential* nature of the agreements: concessions provided to members are not also available to non-members.

18. Viner distinguished between the potential trade-creating and trade-diverting effects of preferential trading arrangements. Trade creation occurs when a lowered barrier between member countries results in one of these countries importing goods that otherwise would be produced at home (or not produced at all). Trade diversion occurs when the preferential treatment causes a country to replace imports from the rest of the world with imports from a partner country. Viner noted that trade creation generates efficiency gains for the member countries, inasmuch as it encourages goods to be produced wherever costs are lowest within the RTA. It can also benefit outsiders—by increasing demand for related intermediate and final goods. On the other hand, trade diversion can be harmful to the importing country: goods that could be purchased from the rest of the world at a low cost are instead procured from a regional source at a higher cost.

19. More important from our perspective than the effects of an RTA on the well-being of member countries is their effect on the welfare of countries that are *not* party to the particular agreement. After all, the multilateral system exists to promote trade cooperation among the GATT Contracting Parties and to discourage each from taking trade actions harmful to other signatories. If countries

11

harmed only themselves by entering an RTA, this alone would not be cause for concern within, and intervention by, the WTO. But if countries were to harm outsiders by joining an RTA, these outsiders would have a legitimate cause for complaint, and the WTO would be the appropriate forum for airing such a complaint.

20. Potential harm to non-participants in an RTA arises due to trade diversion. When preferential access induces a member country to import from another member instead of importing from an outside source, the outside country suffers a decline in demand for its exports. With rigid prices, this reduced demand can translate into a short-run fall in output and employment. With flexible prices, the reduced demand will spell a deterioration in the outside country's terms of trade. It is therefore incumbent upon the WTO to ensure that any RTAs formed among its Contracting Parties are designed to minimize the potential for trade diversion.

21. The potential for trade diversion is related most directly to the size of the external trade barriers maintained by the member countries. If a country has moderate tariffs and other trade barriers, then relatively few importers will find an incentive to shift their sourcing from outside countries to member countries once preferential access is granted. However, if a country has high tariffs and other trade barriers, then the preference afforded member countries will provide a substantial incentive for importers to look within the region rather than to the rest of the world. This means that the WTO should be more tolerant of RTAs formed among countries with liberal MFN trade policies than those formed among countries with restrictive trade regimes. It also means that a lowering of external barriers is an appropriate concession for countries to make when they wish to form an RTA, inasmuch as this lowering of barriers will reduce the scope for harmful external effects.

22. There are some distinctions between the potential for trade diversion under the two main forms of regional trade agreements. In a customs union (CU), the parties to the RTA maintain *common* external tariffs (CETs). Then, as just discussed, the potential for trade diversion varies with the size of these tariffs. The WTO should enforce the requirement that the external tariff (CET) of the parties to a CU be no higher than the average tariff of these countries prior to the formation of the union. Better still would be an effort to limit external tariffs commodity-by-commodity to the minimum pre-union levels among the partner countries. Enforcement of such a rule would reduce the scope for trade diversion associated with the formation

of a CU and thus would minimize the possibility that the union would bring harm to non-member countries.

23. In a free-trade area (FTA), the potential for trade diversion arises especially from the administration of rules of origin. In an FTA, each country maintains its own external tariffs vis-à-vis the outside world. To the extent that these barriers differ, there is always the incentive to import a good through the country with the lowest barriers. Rules of origin are required in order to prevent such trade deflection. They specify the conditions under which goods are considered to be "regional output" and thereby qualify for preferential treatment under the FTA. Three types of rules of origin are common in FTAs. A rule may specify that non-regional intermediate goods must undergo a "substantial transformation process" within the region in order to qualify for regional preferences. This phrase is usually interpreted to mean that the imported intermediate good must undergo a change in tariff classification heading within the region. Alternatively, rules of origin may require that non-regional inputs account for no more than some specified maximum percentage of the production cost or the transaction value of the good. A rule may also require that some specific process be undertaken within the region, or that some other product-specific technological requirement be met.

24. Rules of origin can cause additional trade in intermediate goods to be diverted beyond what would result solely from the differential tariffs applied to regional and non-regional sources of these goods. Consider, for example, an intermediate good with an MFN tariff of zero. Regional producers would have no reason to source this good from high-cost producers in partner countries in order to avoid payment of the MFN duty. But these producers might nonetheless prefer to import higher-cost regional components rather than lower-cost non-regional components in order to satisfy the rules of origin: That is, the use of regional inputs might make the final good eligible for preferential treatment within the region, when it would not otherwise be so. The scope for this type of trade diversion depends on the size of the regional preferences, the restrictiveness of the rules of origin, and the extent of disparities in external tariff rates among member countries.

25. To minimize the scope for such trade diversion due to the rules of origin, the WTO can encourage partner countries to harmonize their external tariff levels and other trade barriers. Once the levels of protection are the same for countries in an FTA, the rules of origin become superfluous. But before such harmonization

13

occurs, the WTO should insist that the parties to an FTA not use rules of origin to protect regional intermediate goods producers.[4] The WTO should encourage countries to enact rules that are as lenient as possible, since non-restrictive rules will not divert any trade. Moreover it should interpret the "not-on-the-whole higher or more restrictive" clause in Article XXIV[5] as applying to the restrictiveness of rules of origin. For example, it might define the *status quo ex ante* regional content of trade in an industry as the average share of regional value added in the total value of goods traded before the formation of the FTA. Then any rule of origin calling for greater regional content than this *status quo* level would be considered as violating this new understanding of Article XXIV.

26. A necessary complement to trade liberalization is the liberalization of private investment.[6] Policy recommendations must address the growing indivisibility between trade, investment, and technology decisions in today's global economy. This is being recognized in recent fora on plurilateral (OECD), bilateral (BITs), and regional (e.g., NAFTA) trade and investment arrangements. The WTO cannot avoid dealing with the foreign direct investment issue.[7]

27. Indeed, the potential for investment diversion may be as important a concern for the WTO as the potential for trade diversion. An RTA leads to investment *creation* if individuals and firms in a member country choose to invest in their partner country when they otherwise would have invested at home, or not at all. Investment *diversion* takes place if investment in a member country displaces investment in the rest of the world, or when investment by a member country displaces investment that would have been undertaken by a firm from an outside nation. Like trade diversion, investment diversion brings external harm to members of the mul-

---

[4] Córdoba (1996) has carried out a comprehensive analysis of the effects of rules of origin applied to Mexican exports to the United States under NAFTA. He found that 86 percent of Mexican exports to the United States fulfilled the rules of origin. However, when he investigated the pattern of trade at the sectoral level, he found a significant correlation between the use of NAFTA preferences and the restrictiveness of the rules of origin.

[5] This clause is discussed in more detail in paragraph 51 below.

[6] The WTO's 1996 report, *Trade and Foreign Direct Investment*, presents evidence of the dramatic growth in FDI in recent years. The report shows that, between 1973 and 1995, FDI multiplied twelve times, while the value of merchandise exports multiplied eight and a half times.

[7] See WTO (1996). This new report recognizes that "investment is at the heart of the WTO."

tilateral system that are not parties to the particular agreement. This harm may come in the form of reduced demand for labor, reduced demand for complementary inputs, reduced transfer of technology, and reduced rates of return on the non-member's capital. An RTA may also induce non-member countries to invest in the region to acquire duty-free access, thereby diverting investment into the RTA. The WTO has an interest in limiting the scope for investment diversion just as it does in limiting that for trade diversion.

28. Investment diversion is most likely to occur when a member country maintains restrictive barriers to investment from non-member countries while granting preferential access to investments from parties to the RTA. In such cases, investors in non-member countries may lose the opportunity to earn high rates of return within the region. The WTO should therefore seek to ensure that countries making investment concessions as part of an RTA or other type of preferential arrangement do so in the context of a more general liberalization of their rules for foreign investment. Restrictive rules of origin can provide an additional incentive for investment diversion; they may motivate firms to locate their plants producing intermediate goods within the region so as to satisfy these rules. The potential for such diversion also can be minimized, as explained earlier, by ensuring that the rules of origin do not require an increase in the portion of the manufacturing process that must be performed within the region relative to the pre-agreement situation.

DYNAMIC FORCES

29. The discussion up to this point has emphasized the static effects of RTAs—in particular the possibly damaging effects that preferential trade agreements may have on the countries that are excluded from them. Recent economic and political science analysis has identified another potential source of external effects from RTAs that is more dynamic in nature[8]: The formation of RTAs may also have implications for the extent and speed of unilateral trade liberalization by members of the WTO and for the direction of the multilateral trade discussions taking place under its auspices. If, for example, countries that join an RTA become more willing to conduct unilateral trade reforms, or if they become more open to the idea of granting concessions in the context of a multilateral negotiation, then RTAs can be seen as contributing toward a more lib-

[8] Bhagwati and Panagariya (1996)

eral trading system in a dynamic sense. On the other hand, if countries that join an RTA become more reluctant to reduce their external barriers, then this will be a further cause for global concern.

30. Economic and political theory offer reasons to expect either one of these outcomes. Many analysts fear that countries that join an RTA may develop a "fortress" mentality; they may see a strengthened regional market as an excuse for erecting barriers to external competition. This argument finds some support in the classical "optimum tariff" argument for protection. Every country has some incentive to protect its imports in order to improve the terms on which it trades. However, a small country setting tariffs unilaterally will have relatively little monopoly power in world markets, and therefore relatively little incentive to restrain its own import demand. Thus the optimal tariffs for a small country are modest. But as countries band together into regional trading blocs, their collective monopoly power in world markets grows. Optimal tariffs for a bloc of countries acting in concert, within a customs union, will be *higher* than those for individual countries acting alone. The implication is that members in a new or enlarged RTA might become more resistant to trade liberalization than they were before.[9]

31. Regional agreements also might cause national leaders to divert resources and political capital from their multilateral initiatives. The pace of multilateral liberalization will be slowed if the specialists needed to negotiate multilateral pacts are asked to spend their time instead on regional matters. And regional agreements might undermine broad-based political support for a multilateral agreement. This could occur if, for example, an RTA allowed member countries to realize most of the available gains from the exploitation of economies of scale, so that the remaining gains attainable through multilateral liberalization would arise only from specialization according to comparative advantage. Whereas the trading gains arising from the economies of scale benefit nearly everyone, those arising from specialization often entail distributional conflicts among different sectors. Thus, a potential multilateral agreement that might find widespread support if it generated gains from both sources could meet opposition from politically powerful groups if most of the gains from achieving economies of scale already had been realized in an RTA.[10]

---

[9] Krugman (1991).
[10] Levy (forthcoming).

32. Yet regional agreements might at the same time promote faster trade liberalization at the multilateral level. RTAs provide a testing ground for new approaches to difficult trading problems, generating valuable information that could make multilateral agreements more palatable and durable. Also, RTAs provide a means by which countries willing to undertake reform more rapidly can do so without interference from countries that prefer a more deliberate approach. Moreover, countries that prefer a slower pace for liberalization may be induced to change their views if they see themselves being left out of major regional initiatives.

33. There are also two possible ways that RTAs, especially FTAs, may introduce new forces for unilateral liberalization by member countries. Consider, *first*, a country that has a higher tariff than its FTA partner for some good. The domestic price of the importable good is likely to be higher in the more highly protected market. The FTA creates an incentive for producers in the low-tariff country to divert their output from their home market to the more profitable partner market. The FTA gives these producers the duty-free market access that makes this diversion possible. As this diversion occurs, consumers in the low-tariff country will experience upward pressure on the price of domestic goods, and so will increase their demand for imports from the rest of the world. In short, the overall effect of the differential external tariffs, combined with rules of origin, will be to increase demand for imports from outside the region in the low-tariff country while reducing demand for outside goods in the high-tariff country. This means rising tariff revenues in the low-tariff country and falling revenues in the high-tariff country. The government of the high-tariff country will have an incentive to cut its tariffs unilaterally, so as to mitigate this loss of revenue. Such a tariff cut should not generate much political resistance from local producers, because these producers otherwise must face increased competition from producers in the low-tariff country that emerges solely as a response to the differential tariff rates.[11]

34. A *second* possible channel for unilateral liberalization comes from the political pressures exerted by downstream producers in high-tariff countries. Before the formation of an FTA, these producers were protected from their regional rivals in low-tariff countries by the application of MFN trade policy. The FTA eliminates this protection from regional rivals while preserving the rivals'

---

[11] Richardson (1992).

advantage from having access to lower-cost, imported components. The downstream producers in the high-tariff country will find a new reason to lobby their government for lower tariffs on intermediate goods once they face more intense competition from other regional producers.

35. To summarize, economic theory alone cannot tell us whether RTAs are likely to increase or reduce the distortions in the world trading system. From a *static* perspective, RTAs are more likely to enhance world efficiency if their primary effect is to create new investment and trade rather than to divert existing investment and trade. The prospects for this depend upon existing trading patterns among would-be RTA members and the way in which the agreement is structured. The WTO—which has as its mandate the encouragement of trade cooperation and the elimination of negative effects on non-members of RTAs—should have an abiding interest in ensuring that RTAs are structured so as to minimize their potential for trade and investment diversion. In practice, this means ensuring that the common external tariffs of a CU and the rules of origin of an FTA do not increase distortions in trade with the rest of the world. From a *dynamic* perspective, the key question is whether RTAs promote or retard further liberalization at the multilateral level. Not much is yet known about which outcome is more likely, but the WTO must be ever-vigilant that RTAs not be used in a discriminatory way, as substitutes for global agreements.

IV. EMPIRICAL CONSIDERATIONS

Like the theoretical literature, existing empirical analysis provides ambiguous answers on the desirability of RTAs. Since most RTAs are likely to generate both trade-creating and trade-diverting effects, it is difficult to isolate the magnitudes of the individual effects from their aggregate impact on trade. Moreover, trade patterns also respond to shocks and stimuli not directly related to the economics of RTAs. In the short-term, these effects may even dominate the trade flow impacts of RTAs.

37. The overall increase in the global volume of trade that has occurred concurrently with the formation of many RTAs complicates the analysis of trade effects. During the post-World War II period, world trade has increased much more rapidly than income. Over the entire postwar period, while world income has risen sixfold, real world trade has increased twelvefold. This effect is also reflected in the trade to gross domestic product (GDP) ratios of the majority of individual countries, which have steadily increased over the last half century.

38. Many studies of the formation of the European Economic Community agree that there initially was much trade creation and little trade diversion, with agricultural trade a prominent exception. This may be because the original EEC members traded a great deal among themselves even before the CU was formed, indicating that each country was the others' low-cost supplier of many goods. However, the subsequent results from EEC expansion are more mixed. Some analysts have found the trade creation resulting from accessions to the EEC to be many times larger than the trade diversion. But significant amounts of trade diversion may have occurred nonetheless. Econometric analysis[12] of the bilateral trade volumes of the European countries finds a negative and statistically signif-

---

[12] Wei and Frankel (1995).

Trade Concentration Ratios: The Methodology

The Princeton Workshop on Policy Issues in International Trade calculated a double-relative statistic, denoted the "trade concentration ratio" (TCR). The TCR measures the relative importance or intensity of the region as a partner for trade generated within the region versus the relative importance or intensity of the region as a partner for trade generated outside the region. Intuitively, the export intensity measure (*XIntensity*) evaluates whether the RTA is of greater importance as a destination for its own exports than it is as a destination for the rest of the world's exports. Similarly, the import intensity measure (*MIntensity*) evaluates whether the RTA is of greater importance as a source of its own imports than it is as a source for the rest of the world's imports. If the importance of the RTA to itself is simply proportional to its importance to the rest of the world, the TCR will equal one. While it is difficult to make a normative *a priori* assertion whether, say, a TCR greater than one is better or worse than a TCR of less than one, this statistic allows for a more thorough examination of what effects the introduction of an RTA has over time.

The components of the TCR can also be evaluated. For example, an increase in the TCR can arise either because (1) the RTA members become relatively more important in members' trade, or because (2) the RTA members become relatively less important in the rest of the world's trade, or (3) both.

Case 1 suggests that there is some trade creation among members, but offers little evidence that the RTA has generated trade diversion, since the RTA's importance to the rest of the world has remained unchanged (although diversion may have occurred anyway).

Case 2 suggests that the rest of the world has been harmed by the formation of the RTA, since the importance of the region to the rest of the world has declined. Such might be the case if the RTA raised barriers to trade with non-members. However, since in this case the region has not become a more important trade partner for the members themselves, there is little evidence of any trade creation at all.

To the extent that nations would only be expected to negotiate RTAs where there was the prospect of some welfare gain, it seems unlikely that a situation that left the parties in an unchanged relationship but harmed external nations would be common. Case 2 scenarios seem more likely to be caused by factors exogenous to the RTA, such as embargoes or oil or transportation shocks, which reduce the desirability of extra-regional trade.

Case 3 provides the strongest evidence of trade diversion. In this situation, the RTA has become more important in the members' trade while at the same time it has become less important in world trade. This suggests, though not conclusively, that increased trade within the RTA is occurring at the expense of trade with third parties.

Table 1. The Princeton Workshop Sample:
RTA Membership, Agreement Type, and Specific Clause

RTA	Membership	Agreement Type (Specific Clause)
EEC/EU (1958)	Belgium, France, Germany, Italy Luxembourg, Netherlands	Customs Union (Article XXIV)
(1973)	Denmark, Ireland, United Kingdom	" "
(1981)	Greece	"
(1986)	Portugal, Spain	"
(1994)	Austria, Finland, Sweden	"
GCC (1983)	Bahrain, Kuwait, Oman, Qatar, Saudi Arabia, United Arab Emirates	Free Trade Agreement (Enabling Clause)
Israel-U.S. (1985)	Israel, United States	Free Trade Agreement (Article XXIV)
ASEAN (1991)	Brunei, Indonesia, Malaysia, Philippines, Singapore, Thailand	Free Trade Agreement (Enabling Clause)
EU-POLAND (1992)	EU Member States, Poland	Free Trade Agreement (Article XXIV)
CEFTA (1993)	Czech Republic, Hungary, Poland, Slovak Republic	Free Trade Agreement (Article XXIV)
NAFTA (1994)	Canada, Mexico, United States	Free Trade Agreement (Article XXIV)
Mercosur (1994)	Argentina, Brazil, Paraguay, Uruguay	Customs Union (Enabling Clause)

icant downward shift in trade between members and the rest of the world on the occasions of the expansion of the EEC from six to nine members in 1973 and from nine to twelve members in the early 1980s.

39. The trade groupings in the Western Hemisphere have not been in existence as long as those in Europe and consequently have received less empirical scrutiny. A recent in-depth study of Canadian and U.S. data, disaggregated by sector, finds little evidence of a negative impact of the Canada-U.S. FTA on the external trade of those countries.[13] It is generally thought that initial U.S. and Canadian tariffs were too low to generate significant trade diversion. The same might not be true, however, of the non-tariff barriers and administered protection (e.g., anti-dumping duties) practiced by these countries.

40. Other recent studies have renewed concern about potential trade diversion resulting from RTAs. For example, Frankel, Kachmeister, Stein, and Wei (1996) compared actual trade among regional groupings from 1965 to 1990 with trade flows projected on the basis of variables such as GDP, distance, and common language. They found that trade within the analyzed regions was larger than these variables would predict. This conclusion raises the possibility that RTAs accounted for these greater-than-predicted intraregional trade flows to the detriment of extra-regional trade flows.

41. A Princeton University workshop group[14] has recently calculated a measure of trade concentration (see box) for each of eight selected RTAs (EU, Gulf Cooperation Council, U.S.-Israel, ASEAN, EU-Poland, CEFTA, NAFTA, and Mercosur). In some instances, there appears to have been a significant increase in regional concentration following RTA formation, while in others the evidence is much weaker. On balance, there appears to be some general tendency toward increased concentration levels. However, while these results suggest that RTAs tend to bias trade toward regional partners, the ultimate impact on world welfare remains less certain.

42. Most of the RTAs examined were characterized by increasing trade concentration ratios (TCRs). Greece's 1981 EC accession

---

[13] Clausing, K. (1995), "The Canada-U.S. Free Trade Agreement: Stepping Stone or Stumbling Block?" Harvard University, Ph.D. thesis.

[14] "Much Ado About Regionalism: Policy Prescriptions for the WTO" (1996), by Chris Bodland, Marinn Carlson, Rick Duke, Dinah McCleod, Peter Rodriguez, Mauricio Rubio, and Rob Youngman, Workshop on Policy Issues in International Trade conducted by Jaime Serra at Princeton University.

proves an exception—driven by lower internal trade volumes and higher external trade. Other exceptions are the initial formation of the EEC in 1958, and the 1991 ASEAN expansion. In both of these situations, intra-regional trade was becoming increasingly significant, but the growth in the regions' importance in extra-regional trade greatly outpaced the intra-regional effects. In both cases it is therefore difficult to conclude that there was significant trade diversion.

43. There were three occasions on which a rising TCR was caused by a rise in internal effects (i.e., Case 1: RTA members become relatively more important in each other's trade): Mercosur, CEFTA, and the Israel-U.S. Agreement (see Table 2). Of these, Mercosur's TCR increased by .56 from a high base of nearly 9.0; there was a sharp increase in the importance of regional trade (75 percent), and anemic growth in the trade importance of external countries (9 percent). There is thus some evidence suggesting the presence of diversion.[15] In only one case, EU-Poland, did a region's TCR fall in terms of both regional and external importance (i.e., Case 2: the RTA members become relatively less important in the rest of the world's trade). As would be expected, such cases are not numerous. That the importance of the RTA in external trade fell by 10 percent while the importance of the RTA to its own internal trade fell by only 2 percent may provide some tangential evidence of trade diversion.

44. There were five occasions on which the TCR rose due to both an increase in the region's internal-trade importance and a drop in its external-trade importance (Case 3). As noted earlier, this scenario provides compelling evidence that increased intra-regional trade is occurring at the expense of trade with third parties. RTAs that exhibited these characteristics include the 1973, 1986, and 1994 expansions of the EEC, the Gulf Cooperation Council, and NAFTA. In particular, the 1994 EU accession seems to have sharply increased the TCR, by nearly 60 percent—a change driven by a drop of nearly 44 percent in the importance of the EU in external trade. The Gulf Cooperation Council, too, experienced a sharp drop (almost 62 percent) in the importance of external trade, leading to

---

[15] Yeats (1996). In a recent study, World Bank economist Alexander Yeats suggests that Mercosur has resulted in significant trade diversion. The study estimates that the near-tripling of Mercosur's intraregional trade in recent years is largely a result of high external barriers to trade.

Table 2. Pre-RTA and Post-RTA Trade Concentration Ratios (TCR[a])

RTA (Year)	Pre-RTA (t-3 yrs.)	Year RTA Formed (t)	Post-RTA (t+3 yrs.)	Change[b]
EEC/EU				
1958				
TCR	—	1.992	1.931	-0.061
RTA Trade	—	0.320	0.366	*0.144*
ROW Trade	—	0.161	0.190	*0.180*
1973				
TCR	1.484	1.596	1.722	**0.160**
RTA Trade	0.495	0.522	0.502	*0.014*
ROW Trade	0.334	0.327	0.292	*-0.126*
1981				
TCR	2.844	1.735	1.969	**-0.308**
RTA Trade	0.600	0.484	0.506	*-0.157*
ROW Trade	0.230	0.281	0.259	*0.126*
1986				
TCR	1.937	1.840	2.315	**0.195**
RTA Trade	0.517	0.567	0.584	*0.130*
ROW Trade	0.290	0.320	0.274	*-0.055*
1994				
TCR[c]	1.260	2.416	2.238	**0.776**
RTA Trade	0.561	0.608	0.620	*0.105*
ROW Trade	0.450	0.253	0.253	*-0.438*

RTA trade=Relative importance of RTA members in members' trade.

ROW trade=Relative importance of RTA members in the rest of the world's trade.

[a]Trade Concentration Ratio: TCR=(Σ[member exports to the region]/ Σ[member exports to the world])/(Σ[rest of world exports to the region]/ Σ[rest of world exports to the world]).

[b]Change reported for *TCR* as *TCR(t+3)-TCR(t-3)*; for Importance in RTA and ROW trade, change reported as percentage change:
 [Importance in Trade (t+3)-Importance in Trade(t-3)]/Importance in Trade (t-3)].

[c]1995 estimate.

[d]1994 estimate.

Table 2. continued

RTA (Year)	Pre-RTA (t-3 yrs.)	Year RTA Formed (t)	Post-RTA (t+3 yrs.)	Change[b]
Gulf Cooperation Council (1983)				
TCR	1.088	1.109	3.301	2.034
RTA Trade	0.048	0.047	0.069	*0.438*
ROW Trade	0.055	0.043	0.021	*-0.618*
Israel–United States (1985)				
TCR	0.082	0.084	0.087	0.061
RTA Trade	0.013	0.016	0.015	*0.154*
ROW Trade	0.157	0.185	0.165	*0.051*
ASEAN (1991)				
TCR	5.565	4.526	3.471	-0.376
RTA Trade	0.177	0.188	0.186	*0.051*
ROW Trade	0.032	0.041	0.053	*0.656*
EU–Poland (1992)				
TCR	1.294	2.125	2.263	0.749
RTA Trade	0.585	0.597	0.573	*-0.021*
ROW Trade	0.282	0.282	0.256	*-0.092*
CEFTA (1993)				
TCR[d]	10.003	13.714	11.143	0.114
RTA Trade	0.090	0.136	0.125	*0.389*
ROW Trade	0.009	0.010	0.011	*0.222*
NAFTA (1994)				
TCR[c]	2.868	3.059	3.158	0.101
RTA Trade	0.384	0.423	0.419	*0.091*
ROW Trade	0.134	0.139	0.133	*-0.007*
Mercosur (1994)				
TCR	8.998	13.156	14.037	0.560
RTA Trade	0.100	0.131	0.175	*0.750*
ROW Trade	0.011	0.010	0.012	*0.091*

a near-doubling of the TCR. The 1973 and 1986 EU expansions both resulted in smaller increases in the TCR; both were about 10 percent. Finally, NAFTA appears to have increased the TCR by only 3 percent, with the importance of the region for internal trade increasing nearly 10 percent. However, both because the drop in the importance of the region in external trade was so small, and because the overall change in the TCR was so slight, the evidence of significant trade diversion is less compelling, although some diversion certainly seems to have occurred.

45. To summarize, empirical studies suggest the same conclusions as theory: Although RTAs do not necessarily bring harm to non-member countries, they are not necessarily benign. This is why it is important that the WTO oversee the formation of these alliances to ensure that the agreements are structured in ways consistent with the broader goals of the world trading community. The trends toward regional integration must be harnessed as a force for global liberalization and kept from impeding further multilateral cooperation. Recognizing that RTAs do not necessarily divert trade, but that they may do so in some cases, and thereby reduce the welfare of non-members, we now turn to an analysis of existing multilateral rules that govern the formation of RTAs.

V. A CLOSE LOOK AT EXISTING MULTILATERAL RULES

Although non-discrimination is a guiding principle of the GATT, the Agreement has always allowed certain exceptions to MFN treatment. The Agreement attempts to limit these exceptions through legal provisions that determine when and under what circumstances such deviations from MFN treatment are permissible. Questions arise as to whether these provisions are effective and to what extent they successfully distinguish between appropriate circumstances and veiled protectionism. This section of our Report examines GATT/WTO rules governing departures from MFN treatment and highlights their ambiguities and weaknesses.

TRADE

47. The GATT sets out two types of exceptions to the MFN rule: general (when Contracting Parties enter into an RTA) and specific (for instance, in the application of safeguards). Logic would suggest that GATT rules and procedures to authorize and mitigate the effects of *across-the-board* exceptions should be at least as (if not more) clear and effective as the legal framework that enables a Contracting Party to invoke more specific GATT provisions that may lead to discrimination. Oddly enough, quite the opposite is true.

48. Whenever the GATT permits a departure from the MFN principle in specific circumstances, it also sets out rules to prevent abuse of the exception or to compensate affected Contracting Parties (see box).

49. From the outset, political considerations led the founders of the GATT to contemplate provisions that would ensure the maintenance and future establishment of regional integration agreements otherwise inconsistent with the MFN obligation of Article I. Initially, the GATT "grandfather clause" and Articles XXIV and XXV provided the necessary legal grounds for certain arrange-

Rules to Prevent Abuse of Specific Exceptions to MFN

Classification of goods. GATT Article I (MFN) applies to trade in "like products." However, the determination of what constitutes a like product often hinges on tariff classification. Countries are often tempted to disaggregate their tariff lines so as to restrict preferences on a particular product to a limited number of trading partners. In the event of discrimination on grounds of tariff classification, the aggrieved party may have recourse to negotiations, compensatory adjustment, and dispute settlement.

Quantitative Restrictions (Article XIII). When countries are permitted to use quotas to restrict imports and such quotas are allocated on an other than "first-come, first-served" basis or through an auction, discrimination often arises. Nevertheless, Article XIII of the GATT and the Agreement on Import Licensing Procedures set out detailed and comprehensive rules to prevent such discrimination and to provide transparency in the administration of quantitative restrictions.

Safeguards (Article XIX). Under the escape clause of the GATT (Article XIX), a member country may take safeguard actions to provide temporary relief to industries adversely affected by surges in imports that result from, *inter alia*, tariff concessions. Discrimination will almost invariably arise in this context where the importing country decides to seek relief by directly allocating import quotas on a country-by-country basis. Here again the GATT requires compliance with substantive and procedural requisites for the adoption of safeguards, and it provides for compensation to be paid by the country that takes the measure.

Article XX. Under this GATT provision, a country may take measures otherwise inconsistent with its obligations under the Agreement (a) to protect interests such as public morals; human, animal, or plant life or health; or national treasures; (b) to conserve exhaustible natural resources; or (c) to take enforcement measures regarding such matters as deceptive practices or anti-competitive behavior. Nonetheless, measures adopted under GATT Article XX must not result in arbitrary or unjustifiable discrimination or in disguised restrictions on trade. In other words, the exception itself incorporates a rule of non-discrimination generally consistent with the objectives of GATT Article I.

Article XXXV. Pursuant to Article XXXV of the GATT, individual contracting parties are permitted to deny application of the Agreement to countries at the time of their accession to GATT. Although one may question the political need to maintain this provision, recourse to Article XXXV has not been frequent because it may only be invoked at the time that a country enters the GATT. Moreover, GATT Article XXXV provides for consultations to review its operation in particular cases.

ments to be exempted from the principle of non-discrimination. Later, two more general exceptions to the MFN rule—Part IV (1965) and the Enabling Clause (1979)—were incorporated into the GATT system with the intent of promoting the trade and development of less-developed countries. With no express guidance set out as to their relationship to Article XXIV, the two provisions have generated further confusion and controversy in the discussion on regionalism and multilateralism. In addition to the uncertainty and overlap inherently associated with the proliferation of enabling mechanisms, the rules that govern their use are ambiguous, and the procedures for their enforcement are weak. This has led to a situation where the GATT (and now the WTO) is unable to assert the leadership required to guarantee the long-term effectiveness of the multilateral trading system. The following brief descriptions illustrate our point:

(a) **Historical Preferences**. Paragraph 3 of Article I and Annexes A-F to the Agreement recognize the existence of certain preferential arrangements at the time that the GATT was established. These provisions allowed the pre-existing agreements to stand without subjecting preferences accorded under them to the MFN obligation.[16] Moreover, the Contracting Parties may also agree to exempt an existing regional agreement at the time that one of its members joins the GATT.

(b) **Article XXV**. Paragraph 5 provides for joint action by the Contracting Parties to waive GATT obligations with respect to any party. Initially, Article XXV was applied only in relation to sectoral agreements (coal, steel, and autos). Its more recent application to regional arrangements reveals a trend to extend its scope to matters otherwise regulated by Article XXIV.

(c) **Part IV (Trade and Development)**. Part IV of the GATT (Articles XXXVI, XXXVII, and XXXVIII), dating back to 1965, was intended to support developing countries. It has been argued that it exempts developed countries that grant non-reciprocal preferential treatment to less developed Contracting Parties from the obligation of non-discrimination set out in Article I. To the extent that unilateral concessions fail to meet the

[16] Arrangements that benefited from the application of the historical preferences clause include the Commonwealth Preference System, the Belgium-Luxembourg Netherlands (Benelux) customs union and the French Union.

"substantially all trade" requirement of Article XXIV, developed countries that are parties to trade agreements with less developed countries have resorted to Part IV in order to escape MFN application.[17] In other words, Part IV has been invoked in relation to agreements that fail to comply with MFN and should also be subject to compliance with the conditions set out in Article XXIV. Thus there is not only clear overlap and tension between Part IV and Article XXIV but also controversy as to the effectiveness of Part IV and Article XXV as catalysts to economic development and trade creation.

(d) **The Enabling Clause.** The Decision on Differential and More Favorable Treatment, Reciprocity, and Fuller Participation of Developing Countries, known as the Enabling Clause, resulting from the Tokyo Round of GATT negotiations (1973-79) has further complicated matters. The Clause allows Contracting Parties to grant preferential treatment to developing countries on a non-MFN basis. There is real danger that—by partially overlapping with Part IV and compounding the erosion of Article XXIV—the Clause could become the instrument of choice for escaping the application of the MFN obligation.[18]

(e) **Article XXIV.** Despite the existence of other, more lenient, enabling mechanisms, GATT Article XXIV remains the central GATT provision on regional integration. It deals explicitly with customs unions and free-trade areas as well as with interim agreements leading to both. In fact, most of the legitimate concerns that led to the approval of Part IV and the Enabling Clause might be better served within the confines of

---

[17] Such is the case of the first three Lomé Conventions between the EEC and the ACP group of countries. In the light of sharp disagreement between GATT members on the compatibility of Lomé I, II, and III with the MFN obligation and on the applicability of Part IV, it was argued before the Lomé IV working group that such a Convention would be in conformity with the GATT only if a waiver under Article XXV were granted. Such a waiver was finally accorded in December 1994 for a period to end in February 2000.

[18] A review of the agreements so far notified to the GATT under the Enabling Clause is quite revealing. Not only has the mechanism failed to contribute to economic development and trade liberalization among developing countries; it has also provided a legal cover for agreements that should have been notified to the GATT under Article XXIV. Furthermore, it is now considered that the Generalized System of Preferences (GSP) operates as an implicit waiver under the Enabling Clause. GSP may also retard trade liberalization in some developing countries and cap the potential growth of their more productive sectors.

THE ENABLING CLAUSE

GATT Contracting Parties, Decision of November 28, 1979, on Differential and More Favourable Treatment, Reciprocity, and Fuller Participation of Developing Countries

Following negotiations within the framework of the Multilateral Trade Negotiations, the Contracting Parties decide as follows:

1. Notwithstanding the provisions of Article I of the General Agreement, *contracting parties may accord differential and more favourable treatment to developing countries, without according such treatment to other contracting parties.*

2. The provisions of paragraph 1 apply to the following:

(a) Preferential tariff treatment accorded by developed contracting parties to products originating in developing countries in accordance with the Generalized System of Preferences;

(b) Differential and more favourable treatment with respect to the provisions of the General Agreement concerning non-tariff measures governed by the provisions of instruments multilaterally negotiated under the auspices of the GATT;

(c) Regional or global arrangements entered into amongst less-developed contracting parties for the mutual reduction or elimination of tariffs and, in accordance with criteria or conditions which may be prescribed by the Contracting Parties, for the mutual reduction or elimination of non-tariff measures, on products imported from one another;

(d) Special treatment of the least developed among the developing countries in the context of any general or specific measures in favor of developing countries. . . .

Note: Excerpt only; italics added.

Article XXIV itself. However, difficulties in the interpretation of Article XXIV's provisions and failure to produce a credible track record in the review of the numerous regional agreements submitted to scrutiny under its rules have prevented this Article from becoming a meaningful catalyst for trade expansion in a manner compatible with the world trading system.

50. Of the GATT working parties formed to review each of the 109 RTA agreements notified to the GATT between 1948 and 1995, only 64 completed their reviews; of those 64, only 6 were able to reach a conclusion on the given RTA's compatibility with the conditionality of Article XXIV. In its original form, Article XXIV has suffered from both legal and political weaknesses that have limited its efficacy as a check on RTAs. To date, no GATT decision has

been made requiring governments to alter their RTA, although some of the RTAs are inconsistent with the prerequisites of Article XXIV. Article XXIV does not require legal approval of an RTA. It only requires notification and then change to accommodate the express decision taken by the Contracting Parties; and it is the absence of such decisions that has created the large loophole.

51. Several ambiguities in Article XXIV became immediately apparent in the working-party review process. When the principle of "not on-the-whole higher or more restrictive" was used to evaluate the common external tariffs of a customs union, questions naturally arose as to whether the new common external tariffs and the presumably divergent set of pre-union national tariffs should be compared by using individual tariff-classification headings, or by using average tariffs calculated annually on the tariff level alone, or on tariffs weighted by trade volumes—and whether "bound" or "applied" tariffs should be used. The EEC, for example, calculated a simple arithmetic average of the tariffs that had been negotiated at the time of notification (final duties on 20 percent of the most "sensitive" goods had not been set by the time of working-party deliberations) and refused to engage in any further discussion of calculation methods; in the EEC's view, Article XXIV's failure to specify a measure left that question up to RTA signatories. The review process stalled for lack of consensus. An inconclusive report, the first of many to emerge from working parties, was released; no further challenge was made.

52. The concept of "substantially all trade," which is also at the core of Article XXIV, is equally imprecise and open to subjective legal and economic interpretation. Both principles remain vaguely defined even after the improvements contained in the Understanding of the Uruguay Round. There is still too much room for individual—and therefore discretionary and prejudiced—opinions regarding compliance. In the case of FTAs, the problem is compounded by the fact that there is no specific guideline to assess whether the rules of origin comply with the "not on the whole higher or more restrictive" condition.[19]

---

[19] Nonetheless, and despite its hazy terminology, it is noteworthy that Article XXIV has prompted only three controversies. The lack of controversy may be explained by political-economy arguments: the Article provides governments with "breathing room" to further their own international agendas. For practical purposes, since every WTO member is part of a formal or informal regional arrangement, there seems to be a silent acceptance of Article XXIV's problems.

Article XXIV
Territorial Application-Frontier Traffic-Customs Unions and Free-Trade Areas

1. The provisions of this Agreement shall apply to the metropolitan customs territories of the contracting parties and to any other customs territories in respect of which this Agreement has been accepted under Article XXVI or is being applied under Article XXXIII or pursuant to the Protocol of Provisional Application. Each such customs territory shall, exclusively for the purposes of the territorial application of this Agreement, be treated as though it were a contracting party; *Provided* that the provisions of this paragraph shall not be construed to create any rights or obligations as between two or more customs territories in respect of which this Agreement has been accepted under Article XXVI or is being applied under Article XXXIII or pursuant to the Protocol of Provisional Application by a single contracting party.

2. For the purposes of this Agreement a customs territory shall be understood to mean any territory with respect to which separate tariffs or other regulations of commerce are maintained for a substantial part of the trade of such territory with other territories.

3. The provisions of this Agreement shall not be construed to prevent:

(*a*) Advantages accorded by any contracting party to adjacent countries in order to facilitate frontier traffic;

(*b*) Advantages accorded to the trade with the Free Territory of Trieste by countries contiguous to that territory, provided that such advantages are not in conflict with the Treaties of Peace arising out of the Second World War.

4. The contracting parties recognize the desirability of increasing freedom of trade by the development, through voluntary agreements, of closer integration between the economies of the countries parties to such agreements. They also recognize that *the purpose of a customs union or of a free-trade area should be to facilitate trade between the constituent territories and not to raise barriers to the trade of other contracting parties with such territories.*

5. Accordingly, the provisions of this Agreement shall not prevent, as between the territories of contracting parties, the formation of a customs union or of a free-trade area or the adoption of an interim agreement necessary for the formation of a customs union or of a free-trade area; *Provided* that:

(*a*) with respect to a customs union, or an interim agreement leading to a formation of a customs union, *the duties and other regulations of commerce* imposed at the institution of any such union or interim agreement in respect of trade with contracting parties not parties to such union or agreement

33

shall not on the whole be higher or more restrictive than the general incidence of the duties and regulations of commerce applicable in the constituent territories prior to the formation of such union or the adoption of such interim agreement, as the case may be;

(*b*) with respect to a free-trade area, or an interim agreement leading to the formation of a free-trade area, *the duties and other regulations of commerce* maintained in each of the constituent territories and applicable at the formation of such free-trade area or the adoption of such interim agreement to the trade of contracting parties not included in such area or not parties to such agreement *shall not be higher or more restrictive than the corresponding duties and other regulations of commerce existing in the same constituent territories prior to the formation of the free-trade area, or interim agreement as the case may be*; and

(*c*) any interim agreement referred to in subparagraphs (*a*) and (*b*) shall include a plan and schedule for the formation of such a customs union or of such a free-trade area within a *reasonable length of time.*

6. If, in fulfilling the requirements of subparagraph 5 (*a*), a contracting party proposes to increase any rate of duty inconsistently with the provisions of Article II, the procedure set forth in Article XXVIII shall apply. In providing for compensatory adjustment, due account shall be taken of the compensation already afforded by the reduction brought about in the corresponding duty of the other constituents of the union.

7. (*a*) Any contracting party deciding to enter into a customs union or free-trade area, or an interim agreement leading to the formation of such a union or area, shall promptly notify the Contracting Parties and shall make available to them such information regarding the proposed union or area as will enable them to make such reports and recommendations to contracting parties as they may deem appropriate.

(*b*) If, after having studied the plan and schedule included in an interim agreement referred to in paragraph 5 in consultation with the parties to that agreement and taking due account of the information made available in accordance with the provisions of subparagraph (a), the Contracting Parties find that such agreement is not likely to result in the formation of a customs union or of a free-trade area within the period contemplated by the parties to the agreement or that such period is not a reasonable one, the Contracting Parties shall make recommendations to the parties to the agreement. The parties shall not maintain or put into force, as the case may be, such agreement if they are not prepared to modify it in accordance with these recommendations.

(*c*) Any substantial change in the plan or schedule referred to in paragraph 5 (*c*) shall be communicated to the Contracting Parties, which may request the Contracting Parties concerned to consult with them if the change seems likely to jeopardize or delay unduly the formation of the customs union or of the free-trade area.

8. For the purposes of this Agreement:

(a) A customs union shall be understood to mean the substitution of a single customs territory for two or more customs territories, so that

(i) duties and other restrictive regulations of commerce (except, where necessary, those permitted under Articles XI, XII, XIII, XIV, XV and XX) are eliminated with respect to *substantially all the trade* between the constituent territories of the union or at least with respect to *substantially all the trade* in products originating in such territories, and,

(ii) subject to the provisions of paragraph 9, substantially the same duties and other regulations of commerce are applied by each of the members of the union to the trade of territories not included in the union;

(b) A free-trade area shall be understood to mean a group of two or more customs territories in which the duties and other restrictive regulations of commerce (except, where necessary, those permitted under Articles XI, XII, XIII, XIV, XV and XX) are eliminated on *substantially all the trade* between the constituent territories in products originating in such territories.

9. The preferences referred to in paragraph 2 of Article I shall not be affected by the formation of a customs union or of a free-trade area but may be eliminated or adjusted by means of negotiations with Contracting Parties affected. This procedure of negotiations with affected Contracting Parties shall, in particular, apply to the elimination of preferences required to conform with the provisions of paragraph 8 (a)(i) and paragraph 8 (b).

10. The Contracting Parties may by a two-thirds majority approve proposals which do not fully comply with the requirements of paragraphs 5 to 9 inclusive, provided that such proposals lead to the formation of a customs union or a free-trade area in the sense of this Article.

11. Taking into account the exceptional circumstances arising out of the establishment of India and Pakistan as independent States and recognizing the fact that they have long constituted an economic unit, the Contracting Parties agree that the provisions of this Agreement shall not prevent the two countries from entering into special arrangements with respect to the trade between them, pending the establishment of their mutual trade relations on a definitive basis.

12. Each contracting party shall take such reasonable measures as may be available to it to ensure observance of the provisions of this Agreement by the regional and local governments and authorities within its territories.

Note: Italics added.

TRADE IN SERVICES

53. When the GATT was established nearly fifty years ago, the world's leading economies were *manufacturing* economies. Today, *services* are the predominant sector in these countries. But the rise in services is a world-wide phenomenon, not merely a feature of developed economies. As a result, trade in services comprises an ever-

Table 3. World Trade in Services (U.S.$billions and percentages)

	1980	1993	Average Annual Change(%)
Total Trade in Services	358	934	8.3
OECD[a]	283 (79)	752 (81)	8.6
Rest of World[a]	75 (21)	182 (19)	6.8
Services as Share of Goods and Services(%)	17	22	2.2
OECD	19	23	1.6
Rest of World	13	19	3.5

Note: Data pertain to countries reporting to the IMF.
[a] Percentage shares in parentheses.
Source: World Bank (1995).

increasing share of global trade flows (Table 3). This fundamental change in the nature of global trade was not anticipated in the original Agreement, but it has since been addressed through the General Agreement on Trade in Services (GATS) that resulted from the Uruguay Round.

54. WTO members wishing to depart from the MFN principle of GATS Article II may either include applicable reservations in lists appended to the Agreement, or they may invoke GATS Article V.

55. Article V of the GATS is the equivalent, for services, of GATT Article XXIV and of the Enabling Clause. In many respects, it constitutes an improvement over Article XXIV of the GATT, and it may serve as a model for future revisions of Article XXIV of the GATT and for the work of the WTO Special Committee on Regionalism.

56. Article V of the GATS establishes a requirement to not raise the overall level of barriers to trade in services—within specific sectors and subsectors—beyond the level existing prior to the relevant agreement. This condition is superior to the "not on the whole higher or more restrictive" condition of GATT Article XXIV.

57. Moreover, unlike Article XXIV of the GATT, Article V of the GATS expressly provides for arbitration between parties that fail to reach agreement on the modification of schedules following entry into an RTA by one of them.

FOREIGN DIRECT INVESTMENT

58. Foreign direct investment (FDI), like trade in services, was not addressed in the original GATT. Nevertheless, FDI and trade in both goods and services are complementary activities.[20] Unfortunately, GATT disciplines on investment are insufficient. In today's highly global marketplace, where producers are involved in joint ventures and international networks of affiliates, a safe investment environment has become indispensable.[21]

59. The existing legal framework for foreign direct investment is exceedingly complex and difficult to understand. A broad set of substantive and procedural rules developed by multilateral institutions or set out in bilateral or regional agreements may adversely affect foreign direct investment. In addition to the more than 450 bilateral investment treaties (BITs) reported to date,[22] the present framework includes the OECD Investment Instruments (Codes of Liberalization of Capital Movements and Current Invisible Operations, the National Treatment Instrument, the Draft Convention on the Protection of Private Property, the Declaration on International Investment and Multinational Enterprises); the GATT instruments (TRIMS, TRIPS, and GATS); as well as regional agreements (e.g., the EU treaties and NAFTA). Moreover, different institutions—both national and international—(i.e., the Overseas Private Investment Corporation (OPIC) in the United States, and the Multilateral Investment Guarantee Agency, "MIGA") offer insurance services to

---

[20] The WTO's 1996 report, *Trade and Foreign Direct Investment*, analyzes both the impact of trade policies on FDI and the impact of foreign direct investment on trade. The report concludes that "FDI and host country exports are complementary, and a weaker but still positive relationship holds between FDI and host country imports." See also Blomstrom, Lipsey, and Kylchycky (1988) and Huffbauer et al. (1994) for empirical analysis on Swedish and U.S. experiences, respectively.

[21] The WTO 1996 report previously cited describes the provisions in GATS, the Agreement on TRIPS, the Agreement on TRIMS, the Agreement on Subsidies and Countervailing Measures, the Plurilateral Agreement on Government Procurement, and the dispute settlement rules as an insufficient and non-comprehensive set of rules.

[22] Consider the number of BITs that would be required to approximate the effect of a broad multilateral agreement on investment. The OECD's proposed MAI could render unnecessary up to 325 existing or potential BITs and, in case of subscription by all WTO members, it would be equivalent to 7,140 BITs. This alone would seem to indicate that a multilateral agreement is an option superior to the current free-for-all. Besides, despite their overall similarity, BITs do exhibit some variation, particularly in their exceptions clauses.

foreign investors. In turn, the extent to which host countries adhere to the rules of these institutions greatly depends on considerations of domestic law and on the persuasiveness of the ministries of foreign affairs of the capital-exporting countries or of the MIGA officials. This multiplicity of rules and institutions is making it increasingly more difficult for economic agents that operate globally to compare investment regimes in different countries and regions.[23]

60. Bilateral investment treaties (BITs) are intended to promote the flow of investment between two nations by providing protection from non-commercial risks under international law. In addition, BITs may also provide intellectual property protection. The basic BIT model, developed by the OECD, is a favored instrument among Western Europe's governments. For many years, the Calvo Doctrine, under which foreign investors must waive diplomatic protection and rely solely on local remedies, prevented Latin American countries from entering into international investment protection accords. By the middle of the last decade, however, most Organization of American States (OAS) nations began to accept international arbitration to resolve investor-state disputes. This has resulted in most Latin American nations agreeing to negotiate BITs. By the end of 1995, of the regional total of 32 such treaties, the United States had 9 treaties in the region; Argentina, Chile, and Ecuador, 7; and Venezuela, 5.

61. The OECD has long been involved in the promotion of multilateral legal regimes to promote foreign direct investment. In 1961, it established the Code of Liberalization of Capital Movements and Current Invisible Operations. Fifteen years later, in 1976, it reached a second agreement that included non-binding national treatment commitments in the form of the OECD Declaration on International Investment and Multinational Enterprises. These OECD instruments provide for: national treatment both before and after establishment; repatriation of profits, dividends, rents, and the proceeds of liquidated investment; transparency of regulations; a consultation mechanism to deal with complaints; and peer review to promote the phase-out of remaining restrictions. More recent-

---

[23] The previously cited 1996 WTO report identifies 42 different regional, plurilateral, and multilateral investment instruments: 16 are independent regional instruments; 8 are embedded in other regional frameworks; 7 are plurilateral instruments; and there are 3 binding and 8 non-binding multilateral instruments.

ly, at the beginning of this decade, the OECD determined that these agreements were insufficient and decided to recommend to member nations to begin negotiation of a more comprehensive instrument. In June of 1994, the OECD ministers announced their intention to develop a Multilateral Agreement on Investment (MAI). OECD member nations are working to develop such an accord by spring 1997.[24]

62. In sum, the existing multilateral rules on trade under the WTO umbrella and on investment under various agreements and WTO codes are either incomplete or dispersed and overlapping. No one institution consistently rules on these closely linked issues. These shortcomings weaken the WTO's ability to play a meaningful role in avoiding distortions in global trade in goods and capital.

---

[24] Bosland, et.al. (1996).

VI. POLICY RECOMMENDATIONS

Theoretical and empirical analysis of the effects of trade and investment agreements on the multilateral system does not rule out the possibility of trade and investment diversion. This makes it important to take appropriate precautions to strengthen the WTO's ability to guide the process of regionalization. Yet the WTO is not at present sufficiently equipped to manage the challenges and opportunities presented by this process.

64. In principle, the WTO addresses the formation of RTAs through Article XXIV and other enabling mechanisms, but analysis and experience demonstrate the inadequacy of these clauses. In addition, regional or bilateral investment agreements are outside the WTO's sphere of influence. As a result, trade- and investment-diverting effects of RTAs and other investment agreements have not been sufficiently constrained.

65. The following policy recommendations address this issue. They cover, first, the improvement of Article XXIV; second, the harmonization of trade rules; third, accession issues; fourth, multilateral rules for investment; and fifth, institutional arrangements related to monitoring, dispute settlement, and WTO rulings. These recommendations amount to an ambitious policy agenda. They are offered as guidelines for future WTO decisions and actions. Clearly not all of them can be implemented immediately. But unless changes of this nature are initiated very soon, preferential regional trade and investment liberalization and the establishment of regional monitoring institutions will continue to pose a serious challenge to the WTO's ability to protect and advance the interests of all participants in world trade.

Recommendation 1

The WTO should strengthen Article XXIV to provide precise compliance criteria for RTAs, specifically on the following three topics:
(a) MFN tariffs,
(b) rules of origin, and
(c) transparency and enforcement.

---

66. The Understanding on Article XXIV that resulted from the Uruguay Round of negotiations and the strengthened dispute-settlement provisions accorded in that Round have only to some extent reduced the problem of ambiguity. Now there is an explicit, although still arbitrary, method for comparing pre-agreement and post-agreement tariff levels; time limits for transitions are defined; there are rules for *ex-ante* compensation for movements toward a common external tariff (CET) that raises protection in one or several countries; there are compulsory working-party reviews; and there are automatic dispute-settlement procedures. Nonetheless, basic uncertainties persist, since the principles of "substantially all trade" and "not on the whole higher or more restrictive" are not yet precisely bound.

67. Article XXIV must be viewed as a *process*. Some steps in this direction already have been taken with the establishment of the WTO Special Committee on Regionalism for the purpose of overviewing RTA compliance with Article XXIV. The Committee should organize working parties *before* a regional negotiation begins. Prior to the negotiation of an RTA, WTO input may be helpful in shaping an agreement to make it compatible with the multilateral trade system. Probably more important, early engagement can influence the negotiating parties' objectives and strategies. Similarly, WTO involvement should continue well *after* the creation of an RTA. The implementation of an RTA, whether in its complete or interim form, can be just as critical as its textual foundation. The Trade Policy Review Mechanism now in place could be extended to include review of Contracting Parties' trade RTAs.

MFN TARIFFS

68. The current Understanding on Article XXIV places emphasis on specific criteria to quantify tariff compliance. Leaving aside

the issue of the analytical pertinence of the new criteria, these guidelines are still insufficient, and stricter controls on MFN bindings should be introduced. For example, if a country's bound tariffs are higher than the tariffs it applies before it becomes a member of an RTA, then once the RTA enters into force, the MFN tariff structure can be subject to protectionist pressures.[25] One solution to this problem, based upon applied MFN tariff rates, would be to have the Article state that the tariff bindings in an RTA become MFN bindings, with possible allowance for a transition period. With respect to customs unions, experience has shown (particularly in Latin America) that negotiating this type of agreement from scratch can lead to common external tariffs (CETs) that are higher than the set of minimum tariffs among the partner countries. This result can be interpreted as a violation of the "shall not on the whole be higher or more restrictive" principle. Therefore, in the case of customs unions, Article XXIV should provide stricter guidelines for CET determination. An ideal outcome would be to bind each member's pre-agreement applied tariff levels and allow for a transition toward a minimum CET.

RULES OF ORIGIN

69. This section focuses on preferential rules of origin—those used to grant preferential access within an FTA. As argued above, one simple procedure that avoids trade diversion reasonably well is to define preferential rules of origin that reflect to the greatest extent possible the *ex ante* observed regional content of regional exports. If rules of origin are set more restrictively, i.e., so that they require more regional integration than that observed prior to the establishment of the FTA, trade diversion is likely to result; in this case, the rules of origin are restrictive. Inefficient regional industries have an incentive to lobby for highly restrictive rules of origin. Since consumers and efficient producers from the rest of the world are under-represented, the governments' concern should be to press for non-distorting rules of origin. If negotiators believe it is necessary

---

[25] In the case of NAFTA, for example, Mexico had bound its tariffs before the regional negotiations—most of them at a level of 50 percent. Subsequently, as a result of the Uruguay Round negotiations, the MFN binding was reduced to 35 percent. During the NAFTA negotiations, however, the maximum effective tariff was 20 percent; thus that was the NAFTA binding. The difference between 35 and 20 is the range for MFN tariff increases consistent with the letter but not the spirit of Article XXIV.

Uruguay Round
Understanding on the Interpretation of Article XXIV of the General Agreement on Tariffs and Trade 1994

. . . Article XXIV:5

2. The evaluation under paragraph 5(a) of Article XXIV of the general incidence of the duties and other regulations of commerce applicable before and after the formation of a customs union shall in respect of duties and charges be based upon *an overall assessment of weighted average tariff rates and of customs duties collected*. This assessment shall be based on import statistics for a previous representative period to be supplied by the customs union, on a tariff-line basis and in values and quantities, broken down by WTO country of origin. The Secretariat shall compute the weighted average tariff rates and customs duties collected in accordance with the methodology used in the assessment of tariff offers in the Uruguay Round of Multilateral Trade Negotiations. For this purpose, *the duties and charges to be taken into consideration shall be the applied rates of duty*. It is recognized that for the purpose of the overall assessment of the incidence of other regulations of commerce for which quantification and aggregation are difficult, *the examination of individual measures, regulations, products covered and trade flows affected may be required*.

3. *The "reasonable length of time" referred to in paragraph 5(c) of Article XXIV should exceed 10 years only in exceptional cases*. In cases where Members parties to an interim agreement believe that 10 years would be insufficient, they shall provide a full explanation to the Council for Trade in Goods of the need for a longer period. . . .

Article XXIV:6
. . . *Review of Customs Unions and Free-Trade Areas*

7. *All notifications* made under paragraph 7(a) of Article XXIV *shall be examined by a working party* in the light of the relevant provisions of GATT 1994 and of paragraph 1 of this Understanding. *The working party shall submit a report to the Council for Trade in Goods* on its findings in this regard. The Council for Trade in Goods may make such recommendations to Members as it deems appropriate.

8. In regard to interim agreements, *the working party may in its report make appropriate recommendations on the proposed time-frame and on measures required to complete the formation of the customs union or free-trade area*. It may if necessary provide for further review of the agreement.

9. Members parties to an interim agreement shall *notify* substantial changes in the plan and schedule included in that agreement to the Council for Trade in Goods and, if so requested, the Council shall examine the changes. . . .

11. *Customs unions and constituents of free-trade areas shall report periodically to the Council for Trade in Goods,* as envisaged by the Contracting Parties to GATT 1947 in their instruction to the GATT 1947 Council concerning reports on regional agreements (BISD 18S/38), on the operation of the relevant agreement. Any significant changes and/or developments in the agreements should be reported as they occur.

Dispute Settlement

12. The provisions of Articles XXII and XXIII of GATT 1994 as elaborated and applied by the Dispute Settlement Understanding *may be invoked with respect to any matters arising from the application of those provisions of Article XXIV relating to customs unions, free-trade areas or interim agreements leading to the formation of a customs union or free-trade area.* . . .

Article XXIV:12

13. Each Member is fully responsible under GATT 1994 for the observance of all provisions of GATT 1994, and shall take such reasonable measures as may be available to it to ensure such observance by regional and local governments and authorities within its territory.

14. *The provisions of Articles XXII and XXIII of GATT 1994 as elaborated and applied by the Dispute Settlement Understanding may be invoked in respect of measures affecting its observance taken by regional or local governments or authorities within the territory of a Member.* When the Dispute Settlement Body has ruled that a provision of GATT 1994 has not been observed, the responsible Member shall take such reasonable measures as may be available to it to ensure its observance. The provisions relating to compensation and suspension of concessions or other obligations apply in cases where it has not been possible to secure such observance. . . .

Note: Excerpts only; italics added.

45

to grant some protection in specific cases, it is preferable to define a more gradual phase-in of tariff preferences than to introduce permanent distortions through restrictive rules of origin.

70. If countries that negotiate an FTA have sectors with very similar protection with respect to the rest of the world, it is unnecessary to embark on a cumbersome and complex definition of rules of origin for goods produced in such sectors. In these cases, trade deflection—to avoid entry through the country with the highest tariff—will not initially be significant. Adopting a region-wide external tariff (a "sectoral" customs union) is a superior option provided that a minimum tariff is adopted. For sector-specific common tariffs to work, however, protection with respect to third countries has to be very similar for both final goods and the most important intermediate goods used in the production process.[26]

71. At present, the WTO does not provide any guideline on how to evaluate the effects of rules of origin on the patterns of trade; moreover, there is no legal basis for initiating formal discussion of such effects, since preferential rules of origin are not mentioned explicitly in Article XXIV and are not considered to be a trade policy instrument. The first step toward remedying this situation should be to adopt a new formal understanding of Article XXIV that rules of origin used to determine preferential access within FTAs should be considered "other regulations of commerce," as defined in part 5(b) of that Article. The understanding should also establish that rules of origin will not be more restrictive than the *status-quo ex ante* regional content of exports.[27] This would preclude a comprehensive harmonization of preferential rules of origin, and different agreements could have different rules.[28] The understanding would imply that, when a given FTA is enlarged, the rules of origin will be redefined so as to accommodate, industry by industry, the smaller regional content observed *ex ante*.

72. The implementation of such an understanding might not be especially difficult. First, its very existence would imply an

---

[26] Wonnacott (1996) suggests this hybrid approach for the NAFTA enlargement.

[27] See Rodriguez (1996) for a formalization of this argument in a model.

[28] In that sense, the economic distortions created by preferential rules of origin could be reduced, but the diversity observed today could not be eliminated. For instance, Vermulst (1994) noted that the European Union has 14 different sets of preferential rules of origin; the United States and Canada, 6 each; and Australia, 5.

increased discipline for countries negotiating an FTA, and flagrant violations would thereby be discouraged. Second, as in the case of customs unions with distorting common external tariffs, transition periods could be established to phase out restrictive rules of origin. Finally, rules for compensation in the case of severely restrictive rules of origin could be introduced; third parties hurt by rules of origin could initiate a dispute and prove that, in the special case being considered, a "more restrictive" regime had been established and damage had occurred because products previously incorporating third-country intermediate goods do not benefit from regional preferences.

TRANSPARENCY AND ENFORCEMENT

73. Perhaps the most serious problem with Article XXIV is that it is weakest where it should be strongest. Article XXIV should generate strict and transparent rules-based RTAs. But it is loosely worded. As noted before, in today's most important RTAs, tariff-based trade diversion seems to be less of a concern than non-tariff-based diversion. Article XXIV could be improved substantially to address this important issue in a constructive and practical way.

74. One avenue to explore is to hook up Article XXIV with the improved codes and rules that resulted from the Uruguay Round negotiations. To assure greater transparency, the hook-up with other WTO rules and procedures would give the Article objective criteria for evaluation. One alternative would be to word the Article so that all WTO disciplines on non-tariff barriers are observed (especially with respect to procedures). This approach would integrate Article XXIV with the multilateral agenda contained in the WTO codes and give the global institution a pivotal role in the process of convergence through an explicit mandate to the Special Committee on Regionalism. It would then be possible to establish compatibility criteria based on the set of rules and procedures followed by RTAs (in the case of non-tariff barriers), as well as on quantitative criteria (in the case of tariff barriers). This would not only greatly facilitate convergence on issues such as harmonization of standards (or mutual recognition) but also significantly enhance the role of the WTO as the overseer of RTA convergence.

75. Article XXIV needs to induce adequate compliance. The WTO's mandate needs to be strong enough to enforce a stricter Article XXIV. One aspect that should be strengthened is the Trade Policy Review Mechanism (TPRM). *Ex ante*, compulsory working-party

evaluations under Article XXIV—which allow the WTO to make recommendations regarding inconsistent provisions in an RTA, and which link the recommendations to the automatic dispute-settlement provisions agreed to in the Uruguay Round—would give the review process substance and credibility. *Ex post*, for purposes of RTA evaluation, the TPRM should be regional in scope, and the principal conclusions of the review process should be made public.

Recommendation 2

As an RTA matures, the trade rules employed by the member countries should be required to converge to a common set of rules. In addition, non-preferential rules of origin should not become more restrictive during the transition period to harmonization.

---

76. Trade deflection may occur—even with a common external tariff in a customs union—when member countries maintain different national trade rules, such as anti-dumping and countervailing-duty codes or technical, health, and safety standards. To avoid deflection, member countries apply national "non-preferential" rules or origin. As an RTA moves toward harmonization of trade rules, the need for non-preferential rules of origin vanishes, minimizing trade distortions.

77. Two examples of how trade rules among RTA members have evolved in this direction relate to anti-dumping policy. In one case (an FTA), New Zealand and Australia have substituted their national anti-dumping codes for regional anti-trust legislation. Similarly, in another case (a customs union), the EU applies a regional competition policy. Moreover, a common anti-dumping law is applied by the EU. In the case of NAFTA, the three partners decided to maintain their national legislation and to develop a regional review procedure that assures exporters due process (NAFTA, Chapter XIX). The future of NAFTA's approach to contingent protection, beyond the protectionist pressures that impeded further progress during the negotiations, depends on the region's ability to develop a common competition policy.[29]

---

[29] See NAFTA, Chapter XV.

78. Although the harmonization of trade rules within RTAs would provide the most benefits, the prospects for immediate harmonization are poor. The proliferation of free-trade agreements, each of which maintains distinct trade rules, suggests that countries place a value on maintaining their own trade rules, or that harmonization is too troublesome or difficult a task to undertake. Since it appears that harmonization is too ambitious at the present time, the best approach for addressing potential conflicts may be to pursue a middle course. Such a course would call for a gradual harmonization. During the transition, domestic trade rules would be enforced by applying non-preferential rules of origin. The European Union provides a good model for such an approach.[30]

79. With respect to non-preferential rules of origin in particular, the Uruguay Round Agreement on Rules of Origin established the goal that all non-preferential rules of origin should be harmonized by 1998. These rules should be clear and predictable and should not create unnecessary obstacles to trade. The work program calls upon the Technical Committee to develop harmonized definitions and methodologies for determining the country of origin of a good. The attainment of the Agreement's objective of harmonization of non-preferential rules of origin should result in more efficient world trade flows by creating one standard set of methodologies and definitions. However, the Agreement does not call upon the Technical Committee to ensure that the definitions and methodologies settled upon are, by some measure, less stringent than those used in different countries before the negotiations.

Recommendation 3

The WTO should require that the architecture and accession conditions of RTAs not have the effect of preventing other countries from becoming members.

---

80. The WTO should develop a model accession clause to be included in all RTAs. Such a clause should articulate the set of WTO disciplines that a potential new member must meet prior to enter-

---

[30] Bosland, et al. (1996).

ing into accession negotiations (e.g., the binding of an effective tariff schedule, compliance with final WTO panel reports against it). Compliance with these conditions should entitle the aspiring member to initiate negotiations.

Recommendation 4

The WTO should develop rules to ensure that RTA investment provisions and other investment treaties do not divert investment.

---

81. The diversity of rules and the differing scope for their application in areas such as liberalization, protection, insurance, and dispute settlement may lead to uncertainty and distortion in the flows of capital. It is necessary to develop a more structured and uniform legal framework applicable to foreign direct investment. A WTO multilateral agreement on investment would provide the crucial benefit of harmonizing investment standards, thereby lowering information costs for potential investors.

82. Such a multilateral agreement on investment should have three basic building blocks: *market access* (e.g., MFN status and national treatment); *protection* (e.g., rules for expropriation of investments, intellectual property rights) and *dispute settlement* (e.g., arbitration rules).

83. With regard to **market access**, trade liberalization programs frequently have been accompanied by concomitant direct foreign investment deregulation. This has been accomplished through the elimination of barriers to entry and performance requirements. In particular, the national treatment principle guarantees foreign investors sector access similar to the most favorable treatment accorded domestic investors. Similarly, the MFN principle guarantees all foreign investors the same treatment.[31]

84. Appropriate definitions of "investment" and "investor" are essential, for they limit the scope and sectoral coverage of the foreign direct investment (FDI) regime. With respect to the definition

---

[31] Many countries still apply exceptions to non-discrimination principles on performance requirements.

of investment, since FDI projects generally involve more that the simple transfer of equity from an external to an internal asset (e.g., such projects often involve complex financing mechanisms, or technology transfer), investment should be defined broadly, so that the disciplines accorded apply to the different ways in which FDI can materialize. As for the definition of investor, given the mobility of international capital and the virtually global nationality of foreign investors, any person who carries out substantial business activity in one or more of the partner countries should be treated as a regional investor, regardless of nationality. The last point is important, since it resolves the issue of "inwardness" with a straightforward and non-discriminatory solution: any foreign investor who locates investment in one of an RTA's partner countries is automatically considered a regional investor.

85. With respect to performance requirements and incentives, RTAs should prohibit their use to promote or regulate FDI flows, since they are a source of distortion and resource misallocation. Performance requirements can also generate non-tariff barriers to trade (e.g., if an external balance condition is imposed on FDI or, more indirectly, if domestic content is imposed on government procurement) and performance incentives can generate "actionable" subsidies (i.e., ones against which formal proceedings may be initiated).

86. With regard to investment *protection*, the basic issues involve compensation rules in case of expropriation and the protection of intellectual property rights. Expropriation rules should include due process and should guarantee prompt, adequate, effective, and freely transferable compensation at fair market value. In addition, a WTO multilateral agreement on investment should build on existing international instruments for the protection of intellectual property rights (including TRIPS). Particular emphasis should be given to enforcement issues.[32]

87. With regard to *dispute settlement*, foreign investors should be granted access to investor-state arbitration to resolve treaty-relat-

---

[32] Mansfield (1995) surveyed U.S. executives and found that the level of intellectual property protection in source countries substantially affects the willingness to make more technologically advanced investments as opposed to building low-tech production facilities or simple distribution networks. The logic is that such protection corrects any free-rider problem.

ed disputes with host governments.[33] However, the effectiveness of arbitration, whether between private parties or with the state, greatly depends on the international instruments that govern its practice and on national attitudes toward the non-judicial settlement of disputes. Although many countries have recently modified their legislation to favor private commercial arbitration, the non-judicial resolution of treaty-related controversies between investors and a state is still controversial in some parts of the world (for example, in Latin American countries that endorse the Calvo Doctrine).

88. The OECD's experience with investment-related issues and current progress in the negotiations would seem to favor it as the preferred negotiating forum. One important advantage of initiating MAI negotiations within the OECD might be—as the organization itself argues—that the nature of present investment instruments also gives a certain guarantee against discriminatory provisions and against the reintroduction of restrictions. Such pressures probably would arise in a start-from-scratch effort within the WTO. This consideration nonetheless must be balanced against the risk of alienating non-OECD nations, which *ex ante* might feel that their concerns are better represented in other fora, such as the United Nations Conference on Trade and Development (UNCTAD).

89. The first item on an ***investment rules policy roadmap*** for the WTO should build on the OECD Multilateral Agreement on Investment (MAI). The WTO should borrow from the OECD's "open-accession" concept; given the extraordinary difficulties inherent in forging consensus among all WTO members, the broader new multilateral agreement should be instituted as a WTO non-compulsory code with open accession. This might facilitate the necessary consensus for its adoption. Ideally, members could reach broad consensus during negotiations, and a large proportion of WTO members would then become charter members of the new accord.

90. A second component of the investment rules policy roadmap should be WTO implementation, for all of its members, of an Investment Policy Review Mechanism (IPRM), as part of the Trade Policy Review Mechanism (TPRM). This would serve two main purposes: (1) monitoring actual investment performance; and (2) promoting accession to the MAI. Both goals would entail consid-

---

[33] Investor-to-investor controversies can of course always be resolved through arbitration by contractual agreement.

erable effort and might not be feasible initially, but the administrative burden would diminish as additional nations acceded to the investment code as a result of the incentives created by a peer-pressure system of reviews.

91. The investment policy roadmap should also contribute to the multilateral negotiations on the liberalization of trade in services. A service provider with a permanent commercial presence in a country other than his/her own becomes, for all practical purposes, an investor in that country. Accordingly, the investment should be protected as such by the MAI, rather than by the GATS. This is a point that the WTO will have to come to grips with in assuming a leading role in the field of investment.[34]

Recommendation 5

The WTO should use its institutional structure and procedures to actively promote compatibility between RTAs and the WTO itself.

---

92. The problems facing the multilateral system cannot be resolved by creating additional institutions and procedures for the settlement of trade disputes. Policy-makers—whether they are at the domestic, the regional, or the multilateral level—generally dread the implications of new international bureaucracies. Existing international institutions (like the WTO) and procedures (like the WTO's Dispute-Settlement Body, DSB) culminate decades of evolution in the direction of a rules-based trading system. More effective than their predecessors, the WTO and the DSB offer a promising potential in the quest to harmonize RTAs and the multilateral system.

93. Nonetheless, there are now several regional trade arrangements with institutions, dispute-settlement procedures, secretariats, committees, and working groups that potentially duplicate the work of the WTO. For instance, of the 24 regional trade authorities that the WTO is currently analyzing, 22 have their own

---

[34] Article I (2-c) of the GATS Agreement still considers *commercial presence* to be one of the four modes of delivery of services. Under the NAFTA, that logic is eliminated: any form of establishment is entitled to protection pursuant to the investment chapter (Chapter 11).

anti-dumping rules, 18 have regulations governing the use of subsidies, 19 have provisions on competition policy, and 12 incorporate dispute-settlement procedures. RTA institutions may threaten the authority of the WTO if they direct member countries to follow the regional rules to the exclusion of the multilateral GATT/WTO structure. The risk of weakening WTO principles is particularly great if RTAs do not follow GATT/WTO guidelines at the time of their inception (e.g., Article XXIV).

MONITORING

94. The recently created WTO Special Committee on Regionalism should play a pivotal role in monitoring the compliance of RTAs with the provisions of Article XXIV. Such scrutiny should extend beyond a mere examination of the original text of an RTA to careful consideration of its negotiating and implementation stages. As suggested earlier, the Special Committee on Regionalism could borrow from the procedures of the Trade Policy Review Mechanism (TPRM) and the Investment Policy Review Mechanism (IPRM) to closely follow RTA implementation and possible amendment.

OPEN FORUM SELECTION FOR DISPUTE SETTLEMENT

95. The WTO should discourage RTA members from adopting closed forum-selection provisions in their agreement; countries that enter into an RTA should always be free to take to the WTO any dispute that calls into question both WTO and RTA rules.[35]

ROSTERS FOR DISPUTE SETTLEMENT

96. The adoption of specific rules for the selection of arbitrators in regional disputes can greatly contribute to harmonizing the operation of the WTO and RTAs. For example, RTAs could either: (1) grant a WTO institution (e.g., the Special Committee on Regionalism) the right to designate a limited number of the pan-

---

[35] Mexico, Canada, and the United States adopted both open and closed forum-selection clauses in their recent RTA. Pursuant to Article 2005(1) of the NAFTA, disputes arising under both the NAFTA and the GATT, or its successor, may be settled in either forum, at the discretion of the complaining party. However, in the case of disputes concerning certain measures related to the protection of human, animal, or plant life or health, or the environment, the defending party can block recourse to the GATT.

elists to be included in the RTA roster; or (2) require that the members of the RTA select the panelists for a particular dispute directly from the WTO roster.

WTO RULINGS ON DISPUTES

97. In many instances, RTAs either incorporate by reference or entirely copy GATT principles. For example, Article 301 of NAFTA states that national treatment for trade in goods shall be granted in accordance with Article III of the GATT; and Article 309 of NAFTA expressly refers to Article XI of the GATT on import and export restrictions. For practical purposes, this means that disputes under Articles 301 or 309 of NAFTA require an understanding of the GATT body of precedents on Articles III or XI, respectively. In any such instance, an RTA panel should be allowed to consult the WTO (e.g., the Appellate Body), or the WTO could decide to submit an opinion to that RTA panel regarding the interpretation and application of the relevant RTA provision. This would promote the formation of a uniform body of precedents on such fundamental WTO principles as national and MFN treatment.

WTO DISPUTE SETTLEMENT BODY

98. Finally, the Understanding on Article XXIV has made it clear that the WTO dispute-settlement provisions ". . . may be invoked with respect to any matters arising from the application of Article XXIV." In addition, new WTO-DSB rules regarding the constitution of a panel, the adoption of its report, and the application of compensatory measures would contribute to overcoming any stalemate resulting from possible blocking of the operation of dispute-settlement procedures under the GATT. Together, these changes in scope and operation would greatly enhance the legal prospects for the enforcement of Article XXIV.

VII. CONCLUSION

Regional trade agreements have multiplied dramatically over the past 30 years. Yet neither trade theory nor empirical analysis of this RTA boom has demonstrated conclusively what its trade- and investment-diverting effects will be. The possibility therefore remains that the proliferation of RTAs might create trade and investment diversion that could harm non-member countries and the world trading system as a whole. The WTO is ill-equipped to deal with such developments and therefore probably unable to prevent trade and investment distortions that constrain the emergence of an efficient liberal multilateral trade system.

100. In summary, this Report makes five broad policy recommendations to the WTO for better management of "regionalism" trends in the world trading system. Our recommendations concentrate on the need for a *new* Understanding on Article XXIV that establishes precise rules and conditionality on the MFN tariffs of countries joining RTAs and on the rules of origin of free-trade agreements as well as ensures transparency and an effective enforcement mechanism. Our recommendations also elaborate on accession provisions and trade rules and present a "policy roadmap" for defining multilateral rules for foreign direct investment under the leadership of the WTO. Finally, we suggest a series of institutional arrangements to ensure appropriate compliance with the new rules—and thereby to strengthen the leadership role of the WTO.

101. In the absence of changes of this nature, preferential market access to a limited number of countries within particular regions, the deeper integration that RTAs provide through liberal investment policies, and duplicative regional monitoring institutions pose a serious challenge to the WTO. If the WTO fails to adjust its rules for the formation of RTAs, remains dissociated from the investment arena, and does not establish a clear hierarchy of responsibility on monitoring, dispute settlement, and rulings, RTAs will expand in number and size independently of a multilateral authority. Unless it engages

more fully in these areas, the WTO will not only fail to address the negative external effects of RTAs but will also relinquish its potential role to more robust regional institutions. Fifty years after the creation of the GATT, it is important that the WTO oversee the formation of these alliances to ensure that the agreements are structured in ways consistent with the broader goals of the world trading community. The trends toward regional integration need to be harnessed as a force for global liberalization.

ACRONYMS

ACP	African, Caribbean, and Pacific countries (associated with the European Economic Community)
ASEAN	Association of Southeast Asian Nations
BIT	Bilateral Investment Treaty
CEFTA	Central European Free Trade Agreement
CET	common external tariff
CU	customs union
DSB	Dispute Settlement Body
EEC	European Economic Community
EFTA	European Free Trade Agreement
EU	European Union
FDI	foreign direct investment
FTA	free-trade agreement (also area)
GATS	General Agreement on Trade in Services
GATT	General Agreement on Tariffs and Trade
GCC	Gulf Cooperation Council
GDP	gross domestic product
GSP	Generalized System of Preferences
IPRM	Investment Policy Review Mechanism
MAI	Multilateral Agreement on Investment
MFN	most-favored-nation (treatment)
MIGA	Multilateral Investment Guarantee Agency
NAFTA	North American Free Trade Agreement
OAS	Organization of American States
OECD	Organisation for Economic Co-operation and Development
OPIC	Overseas Private Investment Corporation
ROO	rules of origin
ROW	rest of world
RTA	regional trade agreement
TCR	trade concentration ratio
TPR	Trade Policy Review
TPRM	Trade Policy Review Mechanism
TRIMS	trade related investment measures
TRIPS	trade related intellectual property rights
UNCTAD	United Nations Conference on Trade and Development
WTO	World Trade Organization

SELECTED BIBLIOGRAPHY ON REGIONALISM

Anderson, K., and H. Norheim (1993), "History, Geography and Regional Economic Integration," in *Regional Integration and the Global Trading System*. Edited by K. Anderson and R. Blackhurst. Geneva: Harvester Wheatsheaf.

Bachrach, C., and L. Mizrahi (1992), "The Economic Impact of a Free Trade Agreement Between the United States and Mexico: A CGE Analysis," in *The Addendum to Economy Wide Modeling of the Economic Implications of a FTA with Mexico and a NAFTA with Canada and Mexico*. Washington, D.C.: U.S. International Trade Commission, Publication No. 2516.

Bagwell, K., and R. Staiger (1993), "Multilateral Cooperation During the Formation of Free Trade Areas." Washington, D.C.: National Bureau of Economic Research, Working Paper No. 4364.

Bagwell, K., and R.W. Staiger (1994), "Multilateral Tariff Cooperation During the Formation of Customs Unions." London: Centre for Economic Policy Research, Discussion Paper No. 962.

Balasubramanyam, V.N., and D. Greenaway (1993), "Regional Integration Agreements and Foreign Direct Investment," in *Regional Integration and Global Trading System*. Edited by K. Anderson and R. Blackhurst. Geneva: Harvester Wheatsheaf.

Baldwin, R. (1993), "A Domino Theory of Regionalism." London: Centre for Economic Policy Research, Working Paper No. 857.

Baldwin, R., and A. Venables (forthcoming), "Regional Economic Integration," in *Handbook of International Economics*, Vol. III. Amsterdam: North Holland.

Baldwin, R.E., and H. Flam (1994), "Enlargement of the European Union: the Economic Consequences for the Scandinavian Countries." London: Centre for Economic Political Research, Occasional Paper No. 16.

Bhagwati, J. (1992), "Regionalism Versus Multilateralism." *The World Economy*, Vol. 65, No. 3: 730-57.

_____ (1993), "Regionalism and Multilateralism: An Overview," in *New Dimensions in Regional Integration*. Edited by J. DeMelo and A. Panagariya. Cambridge: Cambridge University Press.

Bhagwati, J., and A.O. Krueger (1995), *The Dangerous Drift to Preferential Trade Agreements*. Washington, D.C.: AEI Press.

Bhagwati, J., and A. Panagariya (1996), "Preferential Trading Areas and Multilateralism: Strangers, Friends or Foes?" in *The Economics of Preferential Trade Agreements*. Washington, D.C.: AEI Press.

Blackhurst, R., and D. Henderson (1993), "Regional Integration Agreements, World Integration and the GATT," in *Regional Integration and the Global Trading System*. Edited by K. Anderson and R. Blackhurst. Geneva: Harvester Wheatsheaf.

Bond, E., and C. Syropoulos (1995), "Trading Blocs and the Sustainability of Inter-Regional Cooperation," forthcoming in *The New Transatlantic Economy*. Edited by M. Canzoneri, W.J. Ethier, and V. Grilli. Cambridge: Cambridge University Press.

Bond, E., C. Syropoulos, and L.A. Winters (1996), "Deepening of Regional Inte-

61

gration and Multilateral Trade Agreements." Centre for Economic Policy Research, Discussion Paper No. 1317.

Bosland, C., et. al. (1996), "Much Ado About Regionalism: Policy Prescriptions for the WTO." Princeton University, *mimeo*.

Cadot, O., J. de Melo, and M. Olarreaga (1996), "Regional Integration and Lobbying for Tariffs Against Non-Members." London: Centre for Economic Policy Research, unpublished paper.

Clausing, K. (1995), "The Canada–U.S. Free Trade Agreement: Stepping Stone or Stumbling Block?" Harvard University, Ph.D. thesis.

Cooper, C.A., and B.F. Massell (1965). "A New Look at Customs Union Theory," *Economic Journal*, Vol. 75: 742-47.

Córdoba, J. (1996), "Rules of Origin: The NAFTA Case." Washington, D.C.: World Bank, *mimeo*.

de la Torre, A., and M.R. Kelley (1992). "Regional Trade Agreements." Washington, D.C.: International Monetary Fund, Occasional Paper No. 93.

de Melo, J., A. Panagariya, and D. Rodrik (1993), "Regional Integration: An Analytical and Empirical Overview," in *New Dimensions in Regional Integration.* Edited by J. de Melo and A. Panagariya. Cambridge: Cambridge University Press.

Deardorff, A.V., and R.M. Stern (1994), "Multilateral Trade Negotiations and Preferential Trading Arrangements," in *Analytical and Negotiating Issues in the Global Trading System.* Edited by A.V. Deardorff and R.M. Stern. Ann Arbor: University of Michigan Press.

Dinan, D. (1994), *Ever Closer Union? An Introduction to the European Community.* Boulder, CO: L. Rienner Publishers.

Ethier, W.J. (1996), "Regionalism in a Multilateral World." Department of Economics, University of Pennsylvania, *mimeo*.

Frankel, J., A. Kackmeister, E. Stein, and S. Wei (forthcoming), *Regional Trading Blocs.* Washington, D.C.: Institute for International Economics.

Gatsios, K., and I. Karp (1991), "Delegation Games in Customs Unions." *Review of Economic Studies,* Vol. 25: 133-62.

Grossman, G., and E. Helpman (1995), "The Politics of Free Trade Agreements." *American Economic Review,* Vol. 85, No. 4: 667-90.

Hindley, B., and P. Messerlin (1993), "Guarantees of Market Access and Regionalism," in *Regional Integration and the Global Trading System.* Edited by K. Anderson and R. Blackhurst. Geneva: Harvester Wheatsheaf.

Hoekman, B., and M. Leidy (1993), "Holes and Loophones in Regional Trade Arrangements and the Multilateral Trading System," in *Regional Integration and the Global Trading System.* Edited by K. Anderson and R. Blackhurst. Geneva: Harvester Wheatsheaf.

Hoekman, B., and P. Sauve (1994), "Regional and Multilateral Liberation of Service Markets: Complements or Substitutes." *Journal of Common Market Studies,* Vol. 32, 3: 283-317.

Huffbauer, G.C., and J. Schott (1994), *Western Hemisphere Economic Integration.* Washington, D.C.: Institute for International Economics.

Jackson, J.H. (1991), *The World Trading System: Law and Policy of International Economic Relations.* Cambridge, MA: MIT Press. Fourth printing.

Kehoe, T.J. (1994), "Modelling the Dynamics of North American Free Trade," in *Modelling Trade Policy: Applied General Equilibrium Analysis of a North American Free Trade Area*. Edited by J.F. Francois and C.R. Shiells. Cambridge: Cambridge University Press.

Kemp, M.C., and H. Wan (1976), "An Elementary Proposition Concerning the Formation of Customs Unions." *Journal of International Economics*, Vol. 6: pp. 95-98.

Krishna, K., and A.O. Krueger (1995), "Implementing Free Trade Areas: Rules of Origin and Hidden Protection." Washington, D.C.: National Bureau of Economic Research, Working Paper No. 4983.

Krishna, P., and J. Bhagwati (1993), "Regionalism and Multilateralism: A Political Economy Approach." Economics Department, Columbia University, December 1993. Presented to the NBER Universities Research Conference on International Trade and Regulations. Cambridge, MA, 1993.

Krishna, P., and J. Bhagwati (1994), "Necessarily Welfare-Advancing Customs Unions with Industrialization Constraints: A Proof of the Cooper-Massell-Johnson-Bhagwati Conjecture. Columbia University Working Papers.

Krueger, A.O. (1993), "Free Trade Agreements as Protectionist Devices: Rules of Origin." National Bureau of Economic Research, Working Paper No. 3452.

_____ (1995), "Free Trade Agreements Versus Customs Unions." Washington, D.C.: National Bureau of Economic Research, Working Paper No. 5084.

Krueger, A. O., and K. Krishna (1995), "Implementing Free Trade Areas: Rules of Origin and Hidden Protection." Washington, D.C.: National Bureau of Economic Research, Working Paper No. 4983.

Krugman, P. (1991), "The Move to Free Trade Zones," in *Policy Implications of Trade and Currency Zones*. Edited by Paul Volcker, Federal Reserve Bank of Kansas City.

Lawrence, R.Z. (1991), "Emerging Regional Arrangements: Building Blocks or Stumbling Blocks?" in *Finance and the International Economy*, Amex Bank Prize Essays. Oxford, U.K.: Oxford University Press.

Leamer, E.E. (1994), "American Regionalism and Global Free Trade." Washington, D.C.: National Bureau of Economic Research, Working Paper No. 4753.

Levy, P. "A Political Economic Analysis of Free Trade Agreements." *American Economic Review*, forthcoming.

Lipsey, R. (1957), "The Theory of Customs Unions: Trade Diversion and Welfare." *Economica*, Vol. 24: 40-46.

_____ (1960), "The Theory of Customs Unions: A General Survey." *The Economic Journal*, Vol. 70: 496-513.

Lloyd, P.J. (1982), "3 x 3 Theory of Customs Unions." *Journal of International Economics*, Vol. 12: 41-63.

_____ (1992), "Regionalism and World Trade." OECD *Economic Studies*, No. 18. Paris: OECD.

_____ (1993), "A Tariff Substitute for Rules of Origin in Free Trade Areas." *The World Economy*, Vol. 16, No. 6.

Makower, H., and G. Morton (1953), "A Contribution Towards a Theory of Customs Unions." *The Economic Journal*, Vol. 62: 33-49.

Mansfield, E. (1995), "Intellectual Property Protection, Direct Investment, and Technology Transfer: Germany, Japan, and the United States; International Finance Corporation," Discussion Paper No. 27.

Mayer, W. (1984), "Endogenous Tariff Formation." *American Economic Review*, Vol. 74: 970-85.

McMillan, J. (1993), "Does Regional Integration Foster Open Trade?" in *Regional Integration and the Global Trading System*. Edited by K. Anderson and R. Blackhurst. Geneva: Harvester Wheatsheaf.

Meade, J.E. (1955), *The Theory of Customs Unions*. Amsterdam: North-Holland.

Norheim, H.K., M. Finger, and K. Anderson (1989), "Trends in the Regionalization of World Trade, 1928 to 1990," in *Regional Integration and The Global Trading System*. Edited by K. Anderson and R. Blackhurst. Geneva: Harvester Wheatsheaf.

OECD (1995), *A MAI: Report by the Committee on International Investment and Multinational Enterprises (CIME) and the Committee on Capital Movements and Invisible Transactions (CMIT)*. Paris: OECD, Doc. No. OECD/GD(95)65.

_____ (1995), *Regional Integration and the Multilateral Trading System: Synergy and Divergence*. Paris: OECD.

Palmeter, N.D. (1993), "Rules of Origin in Customs Unions and Free Trade Areas," in *Regional Integration and The Global Trading System*. Edited by K. Anderson and Blackhurst. Geneva: Harvester Wheatsheaf.

Panagariya, A. (1996), "The Free Trade Area of the Americas." *The World Economy*, Vol. 19, No. 5: 485-516.

Panagariya, A., and R. Findlay (1996), "A Political Economy Analysis of Free Trade Areas and Customs Unions," in *The Political Economy of Trade Reform*, Essays in Honor of Jagdish Bhagwati. Edited by Robert Feenstra, Gene Grossman, and Douglas Irwin. Cambridge, MA: MIT Press.

Perroni, C., and J. Whalley (1994), "The New Regionalism: Trade Liberalization or Insurance?" Washington, D.C.: National Bureau of Economic Research, Working Paper No. 4626.

Polak, J. (1996), "Is APEC a Natural Regional Trading Bloc?" *The World Economy*, Vol. 19, No.5: 533-43.

Randall, S.J., H. Konrad, and S. Silverman (1992), eds. *North America Without Borders?: Integrating Canada, the United States, and Mexico*. Calgary: University of Calgary Press.

Richardson, M. (1991), "Endogenous Protection and Trade Diversion." Department of Economics, Georgetown University.

_____ (1992), "Some Implications of Internal Trade in a Free Trade Area." Washington, D.C.: Georgetown University, Department of Economics, Working Paper No. 92-01.

_____ (1994), "Why a Free Trade Area?, The Tariff Also Rises." *Economics & Politics*, Vol. 6 (March): 79-95.

_____ (1995), "On the Interpretation of the Kemp/Wan Theorem." *Oxford Economic Papers*: 47, 696-703.

Rodriguez, P. (1996), "Rules of Origin with Multistage Production." Princeton, NJ: Princeton University, *mimeo*.

Sopiee, N., C.L. See, and L.S. Jin (1987), *ASEAN at the Crossroads: Obstacles, Options and Opportunities in Economic Cooperation*. Kuala Lumpur: The Institute of Strategic and International Studies.

Srinivasan, T.N., J. Whalley, and I. Woolton (1993), "Measuring the Effects of Regionalism on Trade and Welfare," in *Regional Integration and the Global Trading System*. Edited by K. Anderson and R. Blackhurst. Geneva: Harvester Wheatsheaf.

Vermulst, E., P. Waer, and J. Bourgeois, eds. (1994), *Rules of Origin in International Trade: A Comparative Study*. Ann Arbor, MI: The University of Michigan Press.

Viner, J. (1950), *The Customs Unions Issue*. New York: Carnegie Endowment for International Peace.

Wei, S., and J. Frankel. (1995), "Open Regionalism in a World of Continental Trading Blocs." NBER Working Paper No. 5272. September.

Winters, L.A. (1992), "Integration, Trade Policy and the European Footwear Trade," in *Trade Flows and Trade Policy After 1992*. Edited by L.A. Winters. Cambridge: Cambridge University Press.

_____ (1993), "Expanding EC Membership and Association Accords: Recent Experience and Future Prospects," in *Regional Integration and The Global Trading System*. Edited by K. Anderson and R. Blackhurst. Geneva: Harvester Wheatsheaf.

_____ (1995), "European Integration and Economic Welfare in the Rest of the World." Washington, D.C.: World Bank.

_____ (1995), "Regionalism and the Rest of the World: The Irrelevance of the Kemp-Wan Theorem." Washington, D.C., World Bank unpublished paper.

Wonnacott, P., and M. Lutz (1989), "Is There a Case for Free Trade Areas?" in *Free Trade Areas and U.S. Trade Policy*. Edited by J.J. Schott. Washington, D.C.: Institute for International Economics, pp. 59-84.

Wonnacott, P. (1996), "Beyond NAFTA—The Design of a Free Trade Agreement of the Americas," in *The Economics of Preferential Trade Agreements*. Edited by J. Bhagwati and A. Panagariya. Washington, D.C.: The American Enterprise Institute, pp. 79-107.

Wonnacott, R.J. (1990), *Canada and the U.S.–Mexico Free Trade Negotiations*. Toronto: C.D. Howe Institute.

_____ (1996), "Free Trade Agreements: For Better or Worse?" *American Economic Review* Vol. 86, No. 2: 62-66.

WTO Secretariat (1995), *Regionalism and the World Trading System*. Geneva: World Trade Organization.

_____ (1996), *Trade and Foreign Direct Investment*. Geneva: World Trade Organization.

Yeats, A. (1996), "Does Mercosur's Trade Performance Justify Concerns About the Global Welfare-Reducing Effects of Free Trade Arrangements? Yes!" Washington, D.C.: World Bank.

MEMBERS OF THE STUDY GROUP

Jaime Serra was in 1996 the John Weinberg Visiting Professor at the Woodrow Wilson School, Princeton University, and a Distinguished Visiting Associate with the Carnegie Endowment for International Peace. He is now Senior Partner of Serra & Associates International (SAI) in Mexico City. Dr. Serra has served the Mexican government as Secretary of Finance (1994), Secretary of Trade and Industry (1988-94) and Undersecretary of Finance (1986-88). As Minister of Trade and Industry, he was responsible for the negotiation of the North American Free Trade Agreement (NAFTA), the GATT, and the trade agreements entered into by Mexico and Chile, Bolivia, Venezuela, Colombia, and Costa Rica. He was also responsible for designing and implementing Mexican policy in the areas of deregulation, foreign investment, international trade, and intellectual property. Dr. Serra has also taught at El Colegio de México, Universidad de Barcelona, and Stanford University. He has published extensively in major economic journals. Dr. Serra is also the recipient of numerous academic honors, including the Wilbur Lucius Cross Medal from Yale University, where he is now a Trustee.

Guillermo Aguilar Alvarez C. is a Senior Partner of SAI, a Mexico City firm consulting in law and economics. Prior to joining SAI in mid-1995, he was Principal Legal Counsel for the government of Mexico during the NAFTA, G-3 (Mexico, Colombia and Venezuela), Costa Rica and Bolivia free-trade agreement negotiations. In 1984-90, he was Counsel and General Counsel of the ICC International Court of Arbitration in Paris. Mr. Aguilar is a graduate of the Universidad Nacional Autónoma de México (UNAM) School of Law (honors). He has conducted research at the Instituto de Investigaciones Jurí dicas at UNAM and the Centre National de la Recherche Scientifique (France), and he has taught at UNAM, the University of Paris, the University of Montpellier, and the Academy of International Law (The Hague).

José Córdoba is head of Análisis Estratégico Corporativo, a Mexico City consulting firm. Prior to his current position, he was a Senior Trade Advisor to the World Bank. From April 1994 to June 1995, he was Executive Director of Mexico and the Dominican Republic at the Inter-American Development Bank. From December 1988 to April 1994, Dr. Córdoba was chief of staff of the President of Mexico. He previously worked at the Ministry of Planning and Budget as General Director for Economic Policy. Dr. Córdoba has also taught at the University of Pennsylvania and El Colegio de México. He studied philosophy at Université de la Sorbonne, engineering at Ecole Polytechnique, and holds a Ph.D. in economics from Stanford University.

Gene M. Grossman is the Jacob Viner Professor of International Economics at Princeton University. He joined the Princeton faculty in 1980, with an appointment in both the Department of Economics and the Woodrow Wilson School of Public and International Affairs. He has held visiting academic appointments at Tel Aviv University, the University of Stockholm, the Haas Graduate School of Business of the University of California at Berkeley, and the University of Pennsylvania. He has also received numerous professional honors and awards. Professor Grossman has written extensively on international trade issues in such professional publications as the *American Economic Review* and the *Journal of International Economics*. *Innovation and Growth in the Global Economy*, which he co-authored with Professor Elhanan Helpman, was published in 1996. Professor Grossman has served as a consultant to numerous federal agencies and to international organizations, including the World Bank and the Organisation for Economic Co-operation and Development.

Carla A. Hills is Chairman and Chief Executive Officer of Hills & Company, International Consultants. In 1989-93, Mrs. Hills served as United States Trade Representative. As a member of President Bush's Cabinet, she was the President's principal advisor on international trade policy. She was also the nation's chief trade negotiator, representing American interests in multilateral and bilateral trade negotiations throughout the world. From 1983 to 1988, Mrs. Hills was Chairman of the Urban Institute and was a member of the Executive Committee of the American Agenda, co-chaired by Presidents Ford and Carter. In 1981-82, she served as Vice-Chairman of President Reagan's Commission on Housing, and in 1985-86, as a member of the President's Commission on Defense Management. Mrs. Hills earlier served as Secretary of the Department of Housing and Urban Development in the Ford Administration. In 1974-75, she was Assistant Attorney General, Civil Division, United States Department of Justice.

John H. Jackson is the Hessel E. Yntema Professor of Law at the University of Michigan. A member of the Michigan faculty since 1966, he was also Visiting Professor of Law in India in 1968-69, a Rockefeller Foundation fellow (in Brussels, to study the European Common Market), and a research scholar in Geneva at the Headquarters of GATT. Dr. Jackson served in Washington as General Counsel of the U.S. Office of the Trade Representative and has been a consultant for various U.S. government offices and for several foreign governments. He also has been a Visiting Fellow at the Institute for International Economics and Distinguished Visiting Professor of Law at Georgetown Law Center. In 1988-89, he was Associate Vice President for Academic Affairs (International) of the University of Michigan. Dr. Jackson is the author of numerous articles and books, including *World Trade and the Law of GATT*, *The World Trading System: Law and Policy of International Economic Relations*, and *Restructuring the GATT System*.

Julius L. Katz is President of Hills & Company, International Consultants. From 1989 to 1993, Ambassador Katz held the position of Deputy United States Trade Representative. During this period, he was the Chief Negotiator for the United States of the North American Free Trade Agreement (NAFTA). He also had senior management responsibility for bilateral and regional negotiations with Europe and the Western Hemisphere and for the multilateral trade negotiations known as the Uruguay Round. Ambassador Katz previously worked as a public policy consultant and in 1987-89 was Chairman of the Government Research Corporation in Washington, D.C. From 1980 to 1985, he worked in the financial services industry, where he was Chairman of Donaldson, Lufkin & Jenrette Futures, Inc. Ambassador Katz joined the U.S. Department of State in 1950; on his retirement from the Department after 30 years of service, he held the position of Assistant Secretary of State for Economic and Business Affairs.

Pedro Noyola is a Senior Partner at SAI, a Mexico City firm consulting in law and economics. From 1990 to 1994, he served as Mexico's Under-Secretary of Trade and Foreign Investment, and he was Mexico's Under-Secretary of Finance in 1995. He participated in bilateral and multilateral trade and investment negotiations and in the preparation of the new laws related to foreign investment, trade, customs, and tax administration. Dr. Noyola has taught mathematics, economic theory, and applied economics at universities in both Mexico and Spain. He did his graduate work at Stanford University, where he obtained a Ph.D. degree in Engineering. He holds a B.S. from the *Instituto Technólogico y de Estudios Superiores de Monterrey*.

Michael H. Wilson has had a long, successful career that has included senior Canadian cabinet posts in Finance, Industry, Science and Technology, and International Trade. As Minister of International Trade, he secured the North American Free Trade Agreement, guided Canada's GATT negotiations, and pursued Canada's trade and investment interests in 26 countries. He represented Canada at six G-7 Economic Summits, the International Monetary Fund, The World Bank, the Organisation for Economic Co-operation and Development (OECD), and the Asia Pacific Economic Co-operation (APEC). He is currently head of Michael Wilson International (MWI), which he formed after leaving public life in January 1994. He is also Vice-Chairman of R.B.C. Dominion Securities and Director of a number of public companies: Amoco Corporation, Manulife Financial, and Quorum Growth Inc. Prior to his career in public life, Mr. Wilson was an investment banker.

THE CARNEGIE ENDOWMENT
FOR INTERNATIONAL PEACE

The Carnegie Endowment for International Peace was established in 1910 in Washington, D.C., with a gift from Andrew Carnegie. As a tax-exempt operating (not grant-making) foundation, the Endowment conducts programs of research, discussion, publication, and education in international affairs and U.S. foreign policy. The Endowment publishes the quarterly magazine, *Foreign Policy*.

Carnegie's senior associates—whose backgrounds include government, journalism, law, academia, and public affairs—bring to their work substantial first-hand experience in foreign policy. Through writing, public and media appearances, study groups, and conferences, Carnegie associates seek to invigorate and extend both expert and public discussion on a wide range of international issues, including worldwide migration, nuclear nonproliferation, regional conflicts, multilateralism, democracy-building, and the use of force. The Endowment also engages in and encourages projects designed to foster innovative contributions in international affairs.

In 1993, the Carnegie Endowment committed its resources to the establishment of a public policy research center in Moscow designed to promote intellectual collaboration among scholars and specialists in the United States, Russia, and other post-Soviet states. Together with the Endowment's associates in Washington, the center's staff of Russian and American specialists conduct programs on a broad range of major policy issues ranging from economic reform to civil-military relations. The Carnegie Moscow Center holds seminars, workshops, and study groups at which international participants from academia, government, journalism, the private sector, and nongovernmental institutions gather to exchange views. It also provides a forum for prominent international figures to present their views to informed Moscow audiences. Associates of the center also host seminars in Kiev on an equally broad set of topics.

The Endowment normally does not take institutional positions on public policy issues. It supports its activities principally from its own resources, supplemented by nongovernmental, philanthropic grants.